Praise for

Seeing Yourself as Others Do

"The best leaders are aware of their strengths and notable flaws. Change Masters are experts in providing leaders with a tune-up. As both a consumer and a customer of Change Masters since 1995, it's exciting to see that Change Masters is now sharing their insights to executive leadership through this short and wonderful read. In *Seeing Yourself as Others Do*, Change Masters will help leaders see themselves accurately at any stage of their careers."

David M. Ahlers, Chief Human Resources Officer and
Senior Managing Director
GMAC ResCap

"We have seen firsthand the power of using the Change Masters' principles of self awareness and personal reflection. A number of our company leaders have participated in the Change Masters program over the years. We have learned that paying attention to the way we present ourselves to others and improving our communication effectiveness can pay huge dividends in creating a strong team environment. I am glad to see that we are now able to reinforce that message and take it to a wider audience through *Seeing Yourself as Others Do*."

Patrick D. Alexander, Chairman of the Board,
Cold Spring Granite Company

"As an Olympic and head collegiate track and field coach, I know the value of great communication within a team. I highly recommend this book to all college graduates who want to immediately and permanently impact their first roles within the workplace. *Seeing Yourself as Others Do* is a dynamic and innovative approach toward understanding how you are really perceived by others. Every parent of college seniors should buy this book as a graduation gift to maximize their student's chances of getting off to a successful start in their career. I plan to buy a box full and give them out as graduation gifts to the seniors on my teams. This book is simply outstanding!"

Beth Alford-Sullivan, Director of Track and Field/Cross Country
Penn State University
Middle and Long Distance Coach, 2004 USA Olympic Team

"Even the most intelligent leaders will be undermined if they fail to keep self-awareness in the forefront. *Seeing Yourself as Others Do* describes a practical approach to manage how you are perceived. Great leaders will learn how to make the necessary and proper adjustments to improve their own 'authentic executive presence.'"

Richard F. Ambrose, Vice President and General Manager
Surveillance and Navigation Systems
Lockheed Martin Space Systems Company

"Even the most intelligent leaders will be undermined if they fail to keep self-awareness in the forefront."

"My coaching with Change Masters freed me up to lead based on who I really am and to manage myself more effectively moment by moment. Their principles, now captured in *Seeing Yourself as Others Do*, give me the security to adapt along with the wisdom and power to make the difference."

Michael A. Anaya, Sr., FACHE,
Chief Executive Officer
Colorado Plains Medical Center

"This is a highly insightful and empowering book that enables the reader to step back to analyze the cost of inauthentic leadership while concurrently presenting a highly personal, coherent and practical approach to align the inner-self with the outward manifestations of leadership. Each page presents practical and achievable steps to discover one's own unique leadership potential and offers refreshingly upbeat, energizing pointers on confronting and ultimately overcoming our own barriers to achieving our maximum leadership potential. Ultimately, this is a highly optimistic book premised on two underlying beliefs—first, that we have the potential to unlock our own unique, and above all, genuine leadership potential; and second, that our business organizations, clients and customers and, ultimately, society as a whole will value and reward this personal odyssey to authentic leadership."

Robert D. Aronson, Managing Partner,
Aronson & Associates, P.A.

"*Seeing Yourself as Others Do* gives you the unspoken secrets of what makes a good executive. It was a good reminder of what I learned in my coaching sessions with Change Masters. Ambition, good work habits and technical skills are a given, but many do not realize the importance of vocal patterns, body language and just being positive and upbeat with those around you.

We have all seen a content driven manager who failed to communicate in large and small group settings. This book offers practical soft skills that bosses and Human Resources don't often mention and are presumed innate when often they are learned behavior."

David L. Boehnen, Executive Vice President,
Supervalu Inc.

"Not only have Tom and Carol helped over 2,000 people to view themselves through the eyes of others, they have managed to condense and therefore share their key insights through this writing. This compendium of their work demonstrates how executives can benefit by developing a deeper understanding of themselves by practicing the Change Masters' fundamentals. I personally have participated in and benefited from the Change Masters process and have sent many of my valued employees through it as well."

"Those who are going to shape the future owe it to themselves to read this book."

Peter Boynton, Senior Vice President
Amyris, Inc.

"Carlson Companies is deeply committed to leadership development and has been for our entire 70 year history. We have effectively utilized Change Masters to develop our key talent at middle and upper levels. I am very pleased to see this book making their insights more broadly accessible to people in our organization. It's never easy to see yourself as others do, but doing so has never been more important. Those who are going to shape the future owe it to themselves to read this book."

Marilyn Carlson Nelson, Chairman and former Chief Executive Officer,
Carlson Companies

"I have experienced Change Masters personally and sponsored others through the coaching process. Their coaching makes it clear that your actions truly speak louder than your words. *Seeing Yourself as Others Do* is a great book that has successfully communicated the critical aspects of how you need to interact with people every day. It definitely rekindles old memories."

Mike Chabot, Vice President and General Manager,
Cargill Meat Solutions

"I was skeptical that a book could encapsulate the fantastic coaching I had received from Tom and Carol, but they have done a wonderful job in capturing the coaching experience. As a technology architect I find myself in many situations where the soft skills are more important than understanding the technology. This is a must read as a fantastic refresher course for anyone who has used their executive coaching process and a great prerequisite for anyone who is planning on taking their coaching. I found myself applying many of the principles and techniques in this book before I had even finished reading it. This is the perfect book for a business trip."

Larry Clarkin, Technology Architect Fortune 500 Software Company

---

"Change Masters drives real change, not superficial change."

"*Seeing Yourself as Others Do* provides an excellent overview of Change Masters' executive development process which I have found to be extremely effective. In a nutshell, this approach helps leaders understand the impact of their behaviors from the point of view of others. In doing so, we discover how our behaviors at times have unintended results. Through the Change Masters process, leaders learn to purposefully direct their actions in a manner consistent with their intentions to achieve the intended impact in their interpersonal interactions."

Timothy Coats, Vice President World Wide Sourcing,
General Mills

"Change Masters has a disciplined process with clear expectations each step of the way. They use a very candid approach and encourage constructive confrontation relative to the changes needed. Follow up is consistent and impactful in terms of reinforcing specific tactical steps participants need to focus on to address their challenges. They drive real change, not superficial change. Participants clearly identify and address impediments to their effectiveness; there is nowhere to hide. This results in positive change that is clearly identifiable by even the most critical partners. *Seeing Yourself as Others Do* reflects their experience and pragmatic approach."

Charles Daggs, Executive Vice President Sales and CEO, Investment,
Wells Fargo

"Changes Masters' Executive Development Process has made a distinct difference in my career success and my personal life. I sent all of my managers through coaching as well. I am excited about *Seeing Yourself as Others Do* because it brings into focus the understanding of executive presence and how perception is life-altering. The book is a practical guide that provides you with the tools and framework required to make real change and it is now available to anyone wanting to enrich their career."
Regenia David, Assistant Commissioner, Office of Enterprise Technology, State of Minnesota

---

"I've been a client and friend of Change Masters for over fifteen years and have seen dozens of associates and colleagues through the Change Masters process with remarkable results. Keers and Mungavan are truly 'Masters' at their craft. A session with Carol will change your life if it doesn't scare you to death! They have the unique ability to tailor their program to meet the needs of each individual client— no cookie cutter approach here! *Seeing Yourself as Others Do* is a 'must read' for anyone in a leadership position, whether as an aspiring executive or a caring parent. Share it with a friend. They'll thank you!"
Thomas Debrowski, Executive Vice President of Worldwide Operations, Mattel

"No cookie cutter approach here!"

"Change Masters has a unique and effective executive coaching process that I have seen repeatedly deliver significant and positive change. They have been helping executives increase their executive presence for two decades. I am delighted to see Keers and Mungavan capture so many of their tried and true approaches in their book, *Seeing Yourself as Others Do*, so that the great results will now be available to many more people."
Luis de Ocejo, Former Senior Vice President Human Resources, Pillsbury

"A key member of my staff recently completed the Change Masters coaching process. During this time I have observed significant behavior changes in his ability to exhibit executive presence, both in presentations as well as personal interactions. Reading *Seeing Yourself as Others Do* gave me great insight into how Change Masters achieves these major improvements through coaching. I see the book as an excellent way to extend similar improvements to more of my staff. It is easy to read and is jammed full of great ideas that are practical to implement."

Mike Eyerly, Senior Director,
Medtronic

"One of the many areas that struck a chord with me in *Seeing Yourself as Others Do* was remote communications. Most of my interactions with staff are via electronic communications around the world. This book really addresses this critical area of communications and gave me some new practical approaches that I will implement. I have personally experienced the very effective coaching from Change Masters and this book is filled with pragmatic approaches that every leader should learn."

Michael E. Fegley, Vice President of Sales,
Intercontinental Hotels

"No matter what stage you are in your professional career, *Seeing Yourself as Others Do* is a valuable resource. It functions as a mirror, reflecting your true professional self, to help you even more successfully navigate the business environment while also providing insights into the character traits of your colleagues. The principles in this book work for all, but I see a significant opportunity for diverse leaders to accelerate their professional development with this book and with the coaching processes provided by Change Masters. Place purchasing this book at the top of your 'to-do' list."

Mary "Toni" Flowers, Chief Diversity & Inclusion Officer,
Trinity Health

"The work Change Masters does is inspirational and this book captures it all. It is wonderful; one that will stay with me forever as it helps introspection and gives hope. It provides the tools for you to think and work on becoming even better—all in one book. *Seeing Yourself as Others Do* is one of the best companions for any executive who wants to grow."

Natalia Franco, Executive Vice President & Global Chief Marketing Officer,
Burger King Corporation

"The business world is filled with brilliant, ambitious people who often believe that intellectual horsepower will drive their professional success. All too often these great minds wake up wondering why the 'other guy' got the brass ring. *Seeing Yourself as Others Do* should be required reading for those who don't listen and always have to be right. This book and Change Masters will save much heartache and unleash a higher quality of life in terms of your personal and professional relationships. Take the pain now! This book will be tucked into our company handbook for every new employee."

Billy Gamble, President,
Wesco Turf, Inc.

"Being an authentic leader is critical to successful leadership. I have used Change Masters for several of my executives to help them understand their interpersonal impact and give them tools to change. *Seeing Yourself as Others Do* really helps the reader to see how they influence others and the need to be genuine."

Mark Gildea, Senior Vice President,
DaVita

"Change Masters never fails to raise the bar for us at Thomson West and for itself."

"Change Masters has coached me to be much more effective at connecting with an audience when giving presentations to large or small groups and without fear. I have learned to be clear, concise, tell memorable stories, use humor and use silence to deliver more persuasive presentations. Keers and Mungavan have captured in their book, *Seeing Yourself as Others Do,* many of the approaches that were most helpful to me. I would highly recommend this book to those who want to be more powerful in their influence and persuasion effectiveness."

Bjørn Gullaksen, Former President, Regent Luxury Group,
Carlson Hotels Worldwide

"Understanding how you are perceived is absolutely key to being successful as a leader. I was told a number of years ago that I needed more executive presence in order to progress as a leader. No one could tell me what that meant until I went to Change Masters for coaching. They gave me very commonsense and usable approaches that made all the difference and helped me get to higher levels of leadership. *Seeing Yourself as Others Do* captures what was so valuable to me. Read this book to get ready for your next promotion. I know it works."

Gokul Hemmady
Chief Financial Officer
NII Holdings

"The Toro Company has a long and rich history with Change Masters. Having personally worked with both Carol Keers and Tom Mungavan for almost two decades, both as a person who's been through their coaching process as well as a sponsor of others going through the process, it is great to see some of the successful Change Masters' concepts and practices now embodied in their book *Seeing Yourself as Others Do*. The Change Masters experience most certainly helped me on my leadership journey."

"Give this book to one of your growing leaders and you'll see a noticeable improvement."

Mike Hoffman, Chairman & Chief
Executive Officer,
The Toro Company

"This eminently readable and practical book is an essential guide for leaders responsible for mobilizing others to achieve collective success. It would be particularly useful for the recently promoted who have had little time or support to prepare for the work of positive influence."

Peter Krembs
Executive Education Fellow,
University of Minnesota Carlson School of Management

"*Seeing Yourself as Others Do* is a very insightful book, which made me look more objectively at myself from an outside-in approach. I had some real 'I didn't realize that' moments when reading it and I loved the discussion on authentic and courageous leadership. We've used Change Masters successfully to enhance our high-talent leaders. Reading the book helped me see that by using the techniques Change Masters is famous for, there is a great deal more to learn to continue enhancing my skills as a healthcare executive. I wholeheartedly recommend this book, filled with relevant 'how to's,' for everyone with the challenging role of leading hospitals and hospital systems today!"

Jone' Koford
Group President: Growth
LifePoint Hospitals

"I had always been fairly confident about speaking in front of groups and felt I was reasonably good. Then Carol and Tom got hold of me when I first joined the executive ranks about a decade ago. They took my speaking effectiveness in front of large and small groups to a whole new level. I guarantee that reading *Seeing Yourself as Others Do* will make you a better communicator and presenter to groups from one to a thousand! If you wish to create truly effective executive leadership presence, want to build strong, trusting relationships or need to be able to communicate clearly and effectively as part of your job, I strongly suggest you read this book today!"

Kathy Hollenhorst, President
Blackline Marketing,

"Change is constant; even experienced change leaders will dramatically improve their results when they connect authentically to others and themselves. I've seen Carol Keers and Tom Mungavan coach very talented and committed individuals to achieve tremendous increases in effectiveness and terrific energy boosts for the organization. Read *Seeing Yourself as Others Do* to gain proven insights; try their approach—it really works: getting authentic with yourself and others really makes a positive difference."

Mike Jensen, Retired Vice President Global Research and Development,
Procter and Gamble

"The practical, down-to-earth style of *Seeing Yourself as Others Do* is very easy to read with specific examples that are tremendously helpful. It's a great resource on effective communication, style and presence—like giving 20/20 vision to the professional leader."

Dean Junkans, CFA, Chief Investment Officer,
Wells Fargo Wealth Management Group

"Over the last twenty-five years, I have seen Change Masters help many leaders whose intentions and behaviors were misaligned. They have provided leaders with eye-opening experiences and pragmatic changes that effectively re-align their behaviors with their intentions, creating significant performance increases. This book is filled with many valuable Change Masters insights that make this type of change happen."

Susan Kinder, Former President,
American Express Travelers Checks

"Maybe the most engaging and useful book on leadership you'll ever read."

"Change Masters never fails to raise the bar for us at Thomson West and for itself. They now serve up their wisdom and collective experience in *Seeing Yourself as Others Do*, a series of easy-to-read leadership lessons seen through the eyes of senior management. This book is a great addition to their highly effective 1:1 work with senior leaders. The practical examples in this book are perfect for Thomson West's emerging leaders."

Rick King, Chief Technology Officer,
Thomson Reuters

"I can say, with firsthand experience, that *Seeing Yourself as Others Do* provides valuable guidance to become a more authentic and effective leader. Change Masters' leadership coaching program, without a doubt, was one of my most powerful development experiences. I dare say I am a better leader, father and husband as a result. Shortly after my 'graduation', I moved to Singapore to run our Asia Pacific operation, so when I've felt a need for a helpful refresher, I pulled out the advice and feedback I received in the program; I'm always amazed at how insightful and timeless their guidance was. The book is a more complete 'reference book' to help me on my journey, one that I encourage others to explore."

Paul S. Kirwin, President,
Carlson Hotels Worldwide

"I have personally known Carol Keers and Tom Mungavan for a couple decades. I've had the opportunity to work closely with both of them. I encourage you to put *Seeing Yourself as Others Do* on your must read list. It is simple on the other side of complexity. That makes it profound. You'll love it. You'll use it. You'll make an even bigger difference."

Doug Lennick, CEO and co-founder of The Lennick Aberman Group
Former Executive Vice President, American Express
Co-Author of multiple books including Moral Intelligence: Enhancing
Business Performance and Leadership Success, and
Financial Intelligence: How to Make Smart, Values-Based Decisions
with Your Money and Your Life

"*Seeing Yourself as Others Do* may be the most engaging and useful book on leadership you'll ever read. It is a practical guide to understanding that elusive but essential leadership quality of executive presence—what it is, why it's so important and how to get it. There is valuable learning here for executives in any corporate culture, at every stage of their careers. I just wish I'd found this book earlier in my career."

"I just wish I'd found this book earlier in my career."

Siri S. Marshall, Former Senior Vice President,
General Counsel and Secretary,
General Mills

"*Seeing Yourself as Others Do* is a tour de force on how to improve your influence in an organization. Keers and Mungavan have distilled their decades of hard-won knowledge into a book that should be kept on the shelf of every executive for reference when presented with situations where they need to increase their influence within the organization."

Frederick K. Martin, CFA, President & Chief Investment Officer,
Disciplined Growth Investors

"Established leaders and those new to the role will find *Seeing Yourself as Others Do* to be a powerful learning tool for re-invigorating or accelerating their careers. Take one nugget at a time and you will unquestionably be enriched."

David McNally, Author,
"Even Eagles Need A Push" and "The Eagle's Secret"

"Many years ago, Carol Keers and Tom Mungavan coached me to become a better leader as well as business mentor while CEO of Toro. The lasting impact they had on me is reflected powerfully in *Seeing Yourself as Others Do*. This is a book for top flight people who want to reach their maximum potential by managing perceptions. I recommend it strongly to talented individuals at any stage of their careers."

Kendrick B. Melrose, Retired Chairman & CEO,
The Toro Company

"Leadership is not only about how smart you are, how competent you are, how strategic you are, but it is about your ability to get things done with and through others. It is the 'other' part of the equation that many smart, gifted and talented people fail at. In *Seeing Yourself as Others Do*, Keers and Mungavan bring clarity, insight and even a roadmap for being successful in working with those important 'others' in our lives, the co-workers, bosses, clients, customers, the public and our family who are all part of the spheres of influence we operate in. Learning and practicing the lessons from this book are perhaps the keys to success for many talented people who are not experiencing as much success as they are capable of achieving. The secret is understanding how others see us and working with and through others to unleash even more success in our careers and our private and public lives. This book is a powerful and useful reference document for anyone who wants to fully unleash their talents to achieve more."

"Change Masters compelled me to get real with myself and my impact on others."

Artie Miller, Vice President of Human Resources,
Medtronic

"*Seeing Yourself as Others Do* is easy to read and crammed full of useful insights and information. It deserves to be read and re-read many times because new and useful ideas will emerge each time."

James A. Mitchell, Executive Vice President (retired)
American Express Company

"Change Masters is a leader in enhancing executive leadership qualities that creates a win-win for individuals and organizations. *Seeing Yourself as Others Do* will enhance all skill levels, from the emerging executive to the CEO. This book is a compilation of research and decades of Change Masters' experiences that will help develop one's executive qualities. The approaches are practical and easy to incorporate immediately. The book is a genuine must-read for any professional looking to build executive presence."

Steve Mona, Chief Executive Officer,
World Golf Federation

"Change Masters compelled me to get real with myself and my impact on others, as well as to scrutinize my own motives, skills and attitudes. Only through that personal shift was I ready to lead an organization through transformational change. Personal transformation is a prerequisite to leading transformational organizational change. The strategies in *Seeing Yourself as Other Do* are powerful accelerators for anyone who aspires to lead personal and organizational change."

Holly J. Morris, Ph.D., Senior Vice President and
Chief Information Officer,
Thrivent

"The coaching that I received through Change Masters is truly the only development program that I have retained and incorporated into my leadership practices. Change Masters helped me to intentionally bring my best thinking to my work and communicate that effectively to a variety of audiences. The work of Change Masters is very holistic and profound in its simplicity. What a useful combination! *Seeing Yourself as Others Do* is practical, applicable, relevant, thought-provoking and down-to-earth."

Lisa Novotny, Vice President Human Resources,
General Mills

"What I especially value about this book, and about Change Masters' approach in general, is the focus on actions—often small actions—that can make a big difference. I also appreciate the way this book is organized; it follows a clear and logical outline. Now that I've read it once, I am certain that I will use it as a reference. *Seeing Yourself as Others Do* is a gem of a book for those looking to improve themselves or coaching others. It is so easy to have others see you differently than you see yourself when you interact with a diversity of people on a daily basis. This book is packed full of useful insights about behavior and very pragmatic suggestions for improving how others perceive you. I highly recommend this book to anyone looking for either a quick read that will certainly yield a few 'ah-has' they can act upon immediately or if they want a guidebook they will refer to again and again."

Laura Owen, Vice President, Chief Administrative Officer,
ADC Telecommunications

"I have observed the results of Change Masters' ability to identify and coach the nuances of communications, leadership and mannerisms that highly impact the effectiveness of the individual executive. They customize their coaching so there is strong and practical alignment with the organization's culture and objectives. *Seeing Yourself as Others Do* shares valuable insights about how they achieve their outstanding results."

John Pattullo, Chief Executive Officer,
CEVA Logistics

"*Seeing Yourself as Others Do* is like a tiny magic box that, when opened, reveals a magnificent bouquet of flowers—flowers of a size and scale that are seemingly impossible to have ever fit in the box! The book is jam-packed with explanations, examples and hints that can make an enormous difference in one's communication and perception by others. The book is the perfect augmentation, versus replacement, to Carol and Tom's coaching. It is an inordinately valuable reference on its own and a perfect refresher for the coaching techniques."

Trudy Rautio, Executive Vice President and Chief Financial and
Administrative Officer, Carlson Companies

"The key to success in leadership, communications or any other endeavor is having a strong understanding of 'self' and others around you. In this book you not only learn how to understand these factors but you learn how to become a more effective communicator and influencer. I highly recommend this book to those who spend most of their lives leading others."

Frank Reid III, Senior Vice President Human Resources,
Elsevier Corporation

"I provided emerging leaders with individual coaching from Change Masters with a goal of helping these talented individuals understand how others perceived them. The valuable insights accelerated the development of the leadership and communication skills they needed to establish early credibility and drive exceptional results. This proactive approach significantly shortened emerging leaders' development cycles, helped them achieve their maximum potential, developed next generation talent for the company and drove bottom line business results."

Jeff Rotsch, Executive Vice President, General Mills

"Change Masters helps you understand that there is a mirror and that you control the reflection in that mirror. They blend tough love, compassion and practicality in transferring their experience to help professionals achieve authentic success.

"This book should be part of on-boarding of all new employees to any organization. It helps them understand that the picture they present to the world is critical to their future and the organization.

"Change Masters is truly the only development program that I have retained and incorporated into my leadership practices."

"The book is also going to become part of my graduation gift to all of the 22-year-olds I know who are filled with new energy and ideas, but little experience in how to express them effectively in the workplace."

Becky Roloff, Chief Executive Officer,
YWCA of Minneapolis

"Change Masters helped me understand that I am in the spotlight as a leader. They coached me to appreciate my power of executive presence as a woman from a different culture—without compromising my belief and passion for driving the business. *Seeing Yourself as Others Do* highlights how to maximize your ability to inspire, motivate, listen, engage and be compassionate. I have found the teachings valuable in both my professional and personal life."

Mandana Sadigh, Senior Vice President Finance and Strategy Planning,
Mattel

"This book is crucial for anyone seeking to understand U.S business culture. It equips and prepares you to succeed and thrive in a way that no college business course ever could! Often the chasm between one's own perception of self and that of others interacting with you, particularly in professional/ workplace settings, can be vast; this book bridges that gap. *Seeing Yourself as Others Do* contains critical information with clarity, honesty and without embellishment. It is invaluable, informative, constructive and vital; this should be required reading for leaders and those aspiring to be."

Piyumi Samaratunga, Attorney

"A 'must read' for all executives. *Seeing Yourself as Others Do* brings the real learning experiences of the Change Masters coaching process to a fun-to-read yet practical leaders' manual that can make impactful and life-changing behavioral differences to any leader. Since perception is reality, this is the reference manual for great leadership!"

John M. Staines, Chief Human Resource Officer, Liberty Medical Supply

---

"This book is packed full of useful insights about behavior and full of very pragmatic suggestions for improving how others perceive you."

"At some point in their career, every successful executive has changed their approach based on feedback from others. *Seeing Yourself as Others Do* offers an inspiring and comprehensive approach to accelerating professional development through change. Read this book twice—once to motivate yourself to accept that change is possible and positive, and a second time to take advantage of the tools and techniques to begin the change process."

Mike Suchsland, President, Corp/Gov/Academic at Thomson Reuters

---

"Few of us are lucky enough to understand how others see us. In the past this was an often overlooked part of becoming successful. This book corrects that oversight. Page after page is packed with insights, good advice and practical wisdom that can make each of us better and more successful."

Darrel F. Untereker, Ph.D., VP of Research and Technology, Medtronic

"I have always appreciated and admired the practical yet proven, effective yet efficient coaching offered by the professional people at Change Masters. Now many of the teachings from Tom's and Carol's years of successful work have been put into one place for the benefit of anyone who reads this book —including those of us who could use a 'refresher' from time to time."

Steve Weeks, Vice President, Strategic Planning,
Tennant Company

"Many years ago as a younger entrepreneur I was frustrated by my company's inability to keep pace with my vision and thus feared losing important opportunities. Enter Change Masters. They brought methods to my madness. Tom and Carol invested themselves personally and totally into transforming me and the entire management group into an effective and dynamic leadership team. *Seeing Yourself as Others Do* is a great culmination of two rich careers."

Billy Weisman, Founder,
Weisman Enterprises

"*Seeing Yourself as Others Do* is filled with proven approaches to increased results. I have personally seen the outstanding results they have achieved with individual coaching and major presentations. They really know how to help people connect with their audience to influence and persuade."

Mary Westbrook, Retired Senior Vice President and General Manager,
Vangent

"Tom and Carol invested themselves personally and totally into transforming me and the entire management group."

"One the biggest challenges facing organizations today is developing the full leadership potential of emerging talent. This book is an invaluable resource to developing authentic executive presence, improving communication and interpersonal effectiveness. Give this book to one of your growing leaders and you'll see a noticeable improvement. Give this book to all your up-and-coming leaders, and you'll see a positive impact throughout your organization."

Kevin Wilde, Vice President, Organization Effectiveness and
Chief Learning Officer,
General Mills

"*Seeing Yourself as Others Do* is like taking 100 books and putting them together into my own personal tutorial. I think I am pretty well grounded, but the approach of thinking about yourself through someone else's eyes is enlightening and in some ways less difficult to be more honest."

Lou A. Welter, CFP® CRPC®, Senior Financial Advisor
Ameriprise Platinum Financial Services practice

"I have used Change Masters' coaching with four different companies, several different business functions and many individuals with varying needs. Every engagement has led to successful, lasting outcomes for both the individuals and the companies. It is great to see the Change Masters' pragmatic approach available in their new book *Seeing Yourself as Others Do*. It is easy to read and will certainly have a significant impact upon you and those around you."

Lance R. Wilson, former Chief Information Officer,
Assurant Health

SEEING

EE

ING

YOURSELF

ASOTHERSDO

AUTHENTIC EXECUTIVE PRESENCE
AT ANY STAGE OF YOUR CAREER

CAROLKEERS THOMASMUNGAVAN

SIGNIFICANTPURSUIT
publishers with purpose

ISBN-13: 978-1-60316-251-7
ISBN-10: 1-60316-251-8

Library of Congress Catalog Number: 2008903248

Printed in Canada

First Printing: June 2008
Second Printing: June 2011

15 14 13 12 11   6 5 4 3 2

SIGNIFICANTPURSUIT
publishers with purpose

3500 Vicksburg Ln N, STE 179
Minneapolis, MN 55447 USA
1-888-329-8881 | www.significantpursuit.com

CONTENTS

INTRODUCTION

1

Introduction—Perception is Reality 1
Seeing Yourself As Others Do
Is Critical To Your Success 3
What is Executive Presence? 7
CLEARLI Seeing Yourself as Others Do. 15
Aligning Internal and External Authenticity 18

FOUNDATIONS

2

Communication Foundations 21
Foundation Skill One: Decade Shift Profile 21
Foundation Skill Two:
The Intelligent Impatient Person Profile. 27
V V C—The Total Communication Message. 31
Foundation Skill Three: OPPOV™
The Power of Understanding the Other Person's
Point Of View. 34
S.O.M.E. Adaptations to Communication 36

COMMAND

3

Command of the Room with Charisma 41
Charisma is Not a Gift. 42
Visual Impact 47
Vocal Confidence. 53
Clear, Compelling Content. 57
Managing Physical Stress Under Pressure 61

LEVERAGE

4

Leverage Influence and Power 65
Influence and Persuasion 66
Build Visibility for Strategic Communications 72
Low-Hanging Fruit—Easy Influence Actions 77
Power and Politics 78
Emotional Competence, Influence and
Political Savvy. 86

EXPECTATIONS

5

Expectations, Strategic and Tactical 91
Execution Tactics—Communicating Clear
Expectations and Tough Messages 93
Consequences—The Time Saver 99
Expectation Setting at Home 102
Using Anger to Clarify Expectations. 104
Strategic Communication. 106
Speak the Language of Strategy 108

AUDIENCE

6

Audience Connections 113
Message Preparation 115
The Power of a Great Story. 118
Prepare to Open and Close Memorably 120
Powerful Delivery 123
Audiences Expect to be Entertained 128
Make It Real 130

RELATIONSHIPS

7

Relationship Competence, Locally and Remotely... 135
Knowing How Others See You Around the World .. 135
Remote Communication Effectiveness............ 136
Where Workplace Relationships Go Awry......... 145
Meeting Basics That Make a Difference 146
Trust—Remote and Local....................... 150
Healthy Conflict............................... 154
The Payoffs of Forgiveness 156

LISTENING

8

Listening Engagement.......................... 159
Traits of a Good Listener....................... 160
Visual Look of Listening........................ 163
Listening is Important.......................... 163
Benefits to Great Listening 165
Techniques that Make a Difference.............. 167
Managing Your Time as a Listener 172
Physical Engagement in Listening............... 174
The 90/10 Rule 174

INSPIRATION

9

Inspiration, Motivation and Praise 177
Payoffs of Courageous Praise................... 177
Gracious Recovery From Mistakes 180
Praise Under Pressure......................... 181
The Power of Meaningful Praise 182
The Praise Matrix............................. 190
Inform Your Face! 191
Asking For Help and Surviving 194
Succeeding In Seeing Yourself As Others Do....... 197

ACKNOWLEDGMENTS

Carol dedicates this book to her great-uncle, John Ingvarsson Gilson, a man who proved to her that anything is possible, and the late Senator Janet Johnson for helping make those possibilities come true. Tom dedicates this book to the courageous Change Masters clients who have made the commitment to be authentic leaders. They will make a meaningful difference in the world for all of us, our children and our grandchildren.

We want to thank the thousands of clients and sponsors who have been an integral part of our wonderful journey. We also thank our staff, friends and family who have supported and encouraged us in building Change Masters and birthing this book. It wouldn't have been possible without your faith and all you taught us. Thank you, every one of you.

Confidentiality

We maintain client confidentiality for the individuals we coach. Most names and details of the client stories have been changed. All outcomes reported are true.

C OMMAND

L EVERAGE

E XPECTATIONS

A UDIENCE

R ELATIONSHIP

L ISTENING

I NSPIRATION

1
INTRODUCTION
PERCEPTION IS REALITY

You don't get to vote on how you are perceived. How others see you is their reality, no matter what you might have intended. That's because we judge ourselves by our intentions and others by their behaviors. How others respond to you as a person and a leader will depend entirely on their perception of you.

Do you think you know how you come across to others? Think again. At Change Masters, we've provided individual leadership communications coaching to over 2,000 very talented people in the United States and internationally. Not one of them completely understood how they were impacting others when we started coaching them.

We've all heard the phrase "Perception is reality," yet you'd be amazed how many people believe this concept doesn't apply to them. Ninety-five percent of the time, our clients are stunned when they see themselves on camera or hear their voices. Even though they look in the mirror every day, the person they're looking at on the screen is a surprise to them. As one of our clients said, "My face is a big scoreboard and I never realized how clearly I was posting the score!" It's why our clients had often been unsuccessful in making behavior course corrections despite getting earlier feedback.

The good news is that you have much more control over how you're perceived than you might expect.

The Impact of Blind Spots

You're under tremendous pressure at work. We hear about it every day. According to research reported in *The Wall Street Journal*, the average corporate executive is some 300 hours behind in their workload at any given time. That kind of constant, unrelenting intensity can destroy the perception of authentic leadership communication in a hurry if you are not aware of it, because it's tough to communicate effectively when you're drowning in tasks. This is why it's crucial to have a variety of approaches to actively manage those perceptions in our time-starved workplace.

It is essential to take control and responsibility for your own perception.

By seeing yourself as others do, you can understand your blind spots, perhaps for the first time. When we know our weaknesses, we are able to compensate for them. Blind spots are trickier, because we don't realize they exist. If you look at what gets us into trouble, it's not just our weaknesses; it's also our blind spots. Some claim that if you just expand your strengths, it will take care of everything. There's no question that you need to capitalize on your strengths. However, it doesn't mean you can just ignore your weaknesses and blind spots. You can be doing very well in the majority of your interactions but can still be brought down by the behaviors in your blind spots.

Look In The Mirror!

We've seen the big career price paid when people are oblivious to the key facets of their impact. A lack of awareness of your impact leads to a lack of balance. A lack of balance leads to missed opportunities to influence, persuade, motivate, listen or deliver difficult news effectively.

It is essential to take control and responsibility for your own perception. We found it allows you to accelerate perceived communication leadership maturity by five to ten years. If you are waiting (or hoping) that others will just understand your intent, you are not living in reality. Understanding how you are perceived is like attaching a rear-view mirror to your forehead so you are more consistently aware of how others see you. Because of this, it's not surprising the number of times clients have said the same phrase to us again and again, "I wish I had done this ten years ago!"

At Change Masters, we have found that by giving our clients a clear picture of how they're seen by others, they are able to implement new approaches to better align their behaviors with their intentions. Others are then more likely to accurately understand what they mean.

One of our clients, a Chief Information Officer for an international packaged goods company, expressed it this way, "What I saw on the outside is not at all what I feel on the inside. It's not what's in my heart or my head. I had rationalized to myself that due to the difficulty of my role I could just do whatever I needed to do to get things done. Now I see that there are better ways to deal with people when I am under pressure or angry or uncomfortable. I really thought I could throw away nice manners because I was busy. It was a big mistake on my part." Your behavior creates the perception formed by others. Being aware enough to choose more effective behaviors or communication approaches gives you the power to influence how you are perceived. If you don't understand the power you wield, you are bound to unwittingly abuse it.

Seeing Yourself As Others Do
Is Critical To Your Success

Some people cringe when thinking about seeing themselves as others do. There's no doubt that it can be painful to understand how you're coming across to others, but this is one area where ignorance is definitely not bliss. Others already see you, for better or worse. You are the last to know about your blind spots. Learning what the rest of the world already knows allows you to accurately adjust your behaviors and better communicate your intentions. It shrinks the gap between perception and intent to help you achieve superior results. As our colleague Peter Krembs notes, "Learning about your flat spots can be temporarily jarring, but in that chaos are the seeds for a whole new set of capabilities."

While the way others see you is their reality, it's not set in concrete. You can change how you are perceived. First, you need to see yourself as others do. Then you need to implement pragmatic behaviors and communication techniques that better represent your intent.

> Learning what the rest of the world already knows allows you to accurately adjust your behaviors and better communicate your intentions.

We know from over two decades of experience that professional coaching expands communication and leadership versatility in an accurate and time-efficient manner. We've put thousands of professionals and executives on camera from over 150 companies around the world. We've recorded tens of thousands of hours of tape on individuals and groups in workplace coaching situations. We have conducted tens of thousands of surveys for our customers. As you can imagine, we've seen just about every possible reaction from our highly talented clientele.

This book will share many of the tips we give our clients in the expectation that you will be able to increase your awareness and enjoy some of the benefits that our professional coaching clients have experienced.

Going for the Gold

The winners of an Olympic gold medal are only a fraction of a second faster than the silver or bronze winners. All the competitors in an Olympic race are great performers, yet only one wins the gold. Our professional clients are all very high-talent performers in their organizations. The goal is to give them the ability to go for the gold in their leadership communication capabilities by giving them an understanding of how they're seen, a practical definition of authentic executive presence and pragmatic tools to help them maximize their overall effectiveness. We've found that as you build your own skills and awareness, you greatly enhance your ability to build your bench strength by mentoring others to increased success.

The most capable leaders are the ones who have mastered CPR—courage, persistence and resilience. Over the years, it's become clear that many communication leadership issues we encounter at Change Masters are due to one thing: a lack of awareness about what a particular situation requires. The leaders who have the mature finesse to adjust and fine-tune the nuances of their style and impact are the people we respect, remember and will follow over the hill.

The smallest things you do at this stage in your career can have a disproportionately large impact.

Mundane Moments

It's often the little things that mean a lot in how others perceive you. The smallest things you do at this stage in your career can have a disproportionately large impact. Many talented people miss huge opportunities by assuming everyone understands their intentions in the seemingly minor, mundane interactions they have hundreds of times a day. They just don't give those moments the attention they deserve.

When it comes to obtaining engagement, your innate personality style really doesn't matter very much. According to numerous studies by the Gallup Organization, strong relationships with co-workers and bosses are what make people happy and productive at work. Gallup psychologist James Harter reported that introverts can be as good at this engagement capability as extroverts. Harter found that only 30% of your ability to be engaging with others is based on your individual disposition. A full 70% of your ability to engage with others is based on the hundreds of day-to-day interactions we all have. These mundane moments consist of nuances most people are unaware of in the crush of their day, such as what your face looks like in the hallway, how you sound in a casual aside at the elevator or how you greet your assistant in the morning. You may be focused on plowing through those 300 hours that you're already behind, but others are forming their perception about you on many levels. They could be right—or they could be wrong.

But That's Not What I Meant!

There are times when you've been perfectly understood. There are probably also times where you have been completely baffled by how terribly misunderstood you were when you thought you were completely clear. We know. It happens to all of us, but these misperceptions can be dramatically reduced.

When we record our clients, they are frequently stunned to see a familiar stranger as they watch themselves on the screen. After they receive the perceptual narrative survey data we collect, and re-create everyday situations on camera, the most common reaction we hear is, "But that's not what I meant!" Virtually all of our clients have received 360° feedback in the past and understood the issues at some level, but they've only been told <u>what</u> to do differently, not <u>how</u> to do it. That's what we specialize in: shrinking the gap between intended communications and the message perceived by others. It can be very significant in its impact on executive presence.

As a technology executive noted, after seeing herself as others did in her Change Masters coaching, "I now understand that you can knowingly and unknowingly influence people. Clearly, I need to be more mindful before I open my mouth. For such a marginal amount of effort, I can achieve tremendous incremental growth." You can also achieve executive presence.

What is Executive Presence?

Executive presence is something people often want more of, but have no idea how to obtain. Executive presence is magnetic. It's a seemingly elusive yet powerful personal quality that enables you to achieve superior results; an integration of traits, values, behaviors and actions applied in key situations creating a strong positive impact on the performance and growth of an organization.

We see executive presence representing the choice to show respectful, mature poise while holding people to a higher standard and energizing them in good, bad and ordinary times. It's not easy to acquire, but it is achievable.

We began our journey to find a pragmatic definition of authentic executive presence years ago when a brilliant Indian finance professional came to us for a consultation. We'll call him Vigit.

Vigit had an amazing story. His life had begun in rural India, where his first school was held outdoors under a large tree, sitting on the packed dirt with many other very poor children. He had to walk 20 miles to sit for examinations and win the scholarships that gave him the opportunity to study in the United States. Vigit went on to earn his Masters degree in Business Administration with honors at Harvard University. His résumé was filled with success in blue-chip companies, including the Fortune 500 Company he worked for when we first met him.

Vigit was next in line to be the Chief Financial Officer of his company, but he had a perplexing situation. He'd been told by his CEO that the only thing keeping him from the CFO role was his lack of executive presence. Vigit was baffled by this requirement, so he asked us, "I need to know, how you define executive presence?" It was a crucial question for us because at the time, we had a general definition but didn't know how to give Vigit the specific, practical answer he needed. Vigit's question spurred us to define in behavioral terms the attributes of executive presence that increase effectiveness and success for our clientele.

We researched with clients, interviewed respected executives, searched publications and ultimately found certain common patterns. What became immediately apparent was the fact that there are many different ways to display executive presence. We also found common attributes that we had already been utilizing in our coaching for a number of years. Since Vigit asked his initial question many years ago, we have expanded our coaching services to help people display their innate authentic executive presence. Even our most skeptical, analytical audiences can see a difference. A client who was the head of an engineering group is just such an example. In his follow-up feedback, after his initial Change Masters coaching sessions, he received these encouraging comments from a fellow engineer, "I don't know exactly what executive presence is, but you've definitely got more of something good since your coaching, and it's working great."

By the way, Vigit's story also had a happy ending. He improved so much in his display of executive presence through coaching that he was promoted to the CFO position later that same year.

Who's Got It?

Whom do you see as having executive presence? Often, people tell us names like Colin Powell, Harrison Ford or Oprah Winfrey—actors, talk-show hosts and politicians. These are roles that none of you have, yet all of you have. There are times every day when you need to be politically savvy, when you need to show the engagement of a television personality or when you need to act a role. Don't kid yourself—even the most authentic of us are on stage in the workplace most of the time.

Like Vigit, many professionals are told they "need more executive presence," but are not told what to do about it. Most think executive presence is almost a type of energy, a force field that you palpably feel when people who have it walk in the room. Their strong personality, stature and bearing of confidence and conviction cause people to pay attention when they speak. They give off something in their demeanor that pulls you toward them. People always know when they are in the room. This is a classic description, but it is only one version of authentic executive presence.

For example, a quieter, more introverted client of ours said, "I'm not flashy. I don't talk to hear myself just talk or to hear the sound of my own voice, I talk to make a statement. However, I can see now that to show executive presence, you need to walk into a room so people understand you're the guy because you're coming across as balanced, as having the answers and looking like you know where you're going. You need to let them know that you understand the strategic implications and the tactical commitment it's going to take. That way, they know you see the forest, but you can also let people know what's going on with the trees right now. You learn that it's OK to use emotion in the culture for impact; in fact, you have to do so. You motivate and reward people, but there are also times in a presentation or an interaction when you just have to take a risk to break through and get their attention."

> **Internal authenticity is meaning what you say. External authenticity is saying what you mean.**

Executive presence needs to be authentic to be believed and respected, but it isn't enough for you to know you're authentic on the inside nor is it enough if you just appear externally authentic in your communication and behaviors. It's essential to have both internal and external authenticity to manifest truly authentic executive presence. Internal authenticity is meaning what you say. External authenticity is saying what you mean.

Internal Authenticity

You are the ultimate authority regarding your internal authenticity. Conversely, others are the ultimate authority regarding your external authenticity, because they reflect what others know about you from the outside.

Internal authenticity is based on factors invisible to others: your values, beliefs, principles and purpose. Only you can fully understand if you're being true to yourself. It is when your choices, your values and your behaviors are truly aligned that you have internal authenticity.

There are people who think that being authentic means they can do or say whatever they want under the guise of being authentic. These are the same people who deliver a verbal assault in a meeting and later justify it by saying, "I'm just being honest. I'm only saying what everyone else is thinking. I don't know why you're getting so upset!" This is not authenticity—it's just rudeness coupled with self-centeredness. These people aren't seeing themselves as others do—if they did, they'd know that people saw them as immature and inappropriate.

External Authenticity

External authenticity is based on the visible behaviors others can observe to decide if they think you are authentic or not. We judge ourselves by our intentions, but others on their behaviors. Those who observe and interact with you make constant decisions whether they think you are authentic or not.

Everyone has known inauthentic "empty suits"—people who look the part externally, sound good or are slickly ingratiating but don't deliver results. They're a great example of phony external executive presence without the alignment with internal authenticity. People who can put on a show typically get found out fairly quickly. Business results are a key part of executive presence, so the "empty suit" can only sustain for short periods of time. It is possible for an empty suit executive to get out in front of a moving crowd and look like they are a leader getting results—for a while. However, when there is a lack of alignment between internal and external authenticity, a crisis will expose their underdeveloped flaws with magnificent clarity.

As a result of observing these empty suits, some people are concerned that if they try to show executive presence they'll look shallow or phony, so they go too far in the other direction. Nothing could be further from the truth. When your internal and external self are aligned, you are being your ideal self. When there is a disconnect between your internal and external authenticity, intentions are misunderstood. When there is alignment between your internal and external authenticity, others are able to understand your intentions clearly.

Our goal is to have others' perceptions of our clients be closer to what they truly meant in the first place. The focus of this book and the coaching we do is to provide awareness of any gaps between internal and external authenticity, intentions and perceptions and provide ways to shrink those gaps. That alignment, coupled with mastery of the attributes we'll discuss in this book, is what creates authentic executive presence.

> **Self-awareness is essential to being authentic and understanding your impact.**

Executive Presence Precedes Executive Roles

A *Business Week* study found that 97% of executives believe their performance is in the top 10% of all their peers! What's wrong with this picture? Clearly, this means most executives are fooling themselves, and why wouldn't they? Most don't get objective feedback so they are missing the most valuable information they need: honest feedback.

Self-awareness is essential to being authentic and understanding your impact. You'll be more effective if you are willing to look more objectively at yourself and courageously examine your blind spots. Learning to be more reflective instead of impulsive or reactive allows you to be taken more seriously as a professional by others at any level of your career.

There is a natural learning and maturing process as one matures and takes on more responsibility. Unfortunately, this natural process is often not fast enough for the rising star who is ahead of the normal progression. These high-potential professionals are so talented, but they often missed some critically needed lessons. They were too busy getting great results, only to hit the wall or plateau, typically in their early 40s. It's much harder to learn these early lessons later in life! The reality is that executive skills need to be honed incrementally early in one's career so they are ready when the additional pressure and responsibility of the executive role becomes a reality. Those most effective at demonstrating executive presence started developing it early in their careers.

People with true, authentic leadership presence know how to stay connected with others, even under prolonged stress. You've seen them—the people who're able to stay poised, confident and engaged, even in stressful situations.

These people have executive presence, but most of them weren't born with it. They were wise enough, early on, to know they needed to learn and understand how they're seen by others, which allowed them to build relationships and loyalties for long-term business success. They've managed and led by their authenticity and their power to influence, not by authority or title alone. They created a compelling reason for others to listen to them by effectively reading and meeting the needs and motivations of their audience, no matter what age they were or what title they held.

The greatest leaders we've all known who display executive presence are able to handle multiple demands with grace and apparent ease. They are solidly grounded in values and don't succumb to the enormous pressures they face. After all, nobody wants a nervous airline pilot—or a nervous leader!

The Price of Nice

While most of our clients are initially described as too intense or overwhelming, some fit into our category of clients who are too nice, not having enough "fire in the belly" or who are too hesitant to step up to the tough issues. Overly accommodating behavior eventually gets in the way of the nice person because no one wants to hurt his or her feelings. People can never be sure if they will be supported by the nice person in a crisis situation that requires an assertive or firm approach with others. It is not unusual to see the nice person reach a breaking point and explode in an unexpected venting of frustration, which is a shock to those involved.

Such was the case with Marty. Marty was universally well-liked, but too laid back. He wasn't conveying the necessary urgency or giving the hard feedback without softening it. Meanwhile, his department had quadrupled and the pressure was building.

Marty's boss had these goals for his coaching:

- Increased display of confidence to match his content knowledge.
- Demonstrate 10% more assertiveness at the right times.
- Make a more visible impact in meetings.
- Feel more comfortable with a logical argumentation process so he can lean into the conflict.
- Increase his executive presence—make it easier for people to understand the value he brings to the table.

Marty learned in coaching to incorporate increased confidence and assertiveness coupled with an ability to own his power in meetings. In addition, he embraced the impact of his external appearance and dress on his perceived executive presence. He added a whole new set of communication tools to his already strong relationship skill set.

Here is what Marty told us following his coaching: "You need a poke to get out of your comfort zone. In the past, I was everybody's friend and that's how I got things done. I collaborated with them all and figured the force of the good feelings and relationships I'd created would carry me through. I learned that I needed to be clear and firm about what I needed and expected. When I've done so, I've gained more trust from others. I'm stronger and clearer, but not a jerk. It has been very gratifying to see the results when I stand on my own authority."

Mature Awareness

To obtain this level of awareness, you must be open to feedback. Bill George, former CEO of Medtronic, in his book *Authentic Leadership, Rediscovering the Secrets to Creating Lasting Value*, courageously identified this realization for himself when he said, "I have always been open to critical feedback, but also quite sensitive to it. For years I felt I had to be perfect, or at least appear that I was on top of everything. I tried to hide my weaknesses from others, fearing they would reject me if they knew who I really was. Eventually, I realized that they could see my weaknesses more clearly than I could. In attempting to cover things up, I was only fooling myself."

> **Authenticity in leadership is achieved, in part, by managing yourself more effectively moment by moment.**

Mature leaders who possess executive presence, as Bill George does, have seen themselves as others do. They have accepted that they have weaknesses and have learned to deal with them in a more effective manner by leveraging their strengths more broadly. They know you can't always control the environment around you, but you can always make a choice and control your response to it.

Authenticity in leadership is achieved, in part, by managing yourself more effectively moment by moment. That's why you need to be aware of your impact both internally and externally in order to get the full benefit of your authentic self at work. Executive presence in the boardroom or anywhere else is about how you align and reconcile what you feel on the inside with what others see and hear on the outside. It is based on integrity and good judgment, so that when you do have a dispute, you can weather the disagreement and still have a decent working relationship.

Your choices need to be consistent to be believed and seen as authentic by others. As Robert Fritz said in his book, *The Path of*

Least Resistance, Learning To Become a Creative Force in Your Own Life, "The difference between an amateur and a professional violinist is that amateurs play well when things are going well. Professionals play well no matter what." To show authentic executive presence, you need to be a professional all the time.

CLEARLI Seeing Yourself as Others Do

We have identified seven Authentic Executive Presence attributes that have consistently made a measurable difference in our clients' perceived executive presence. We use the acronym CLEARLI to help you remember these attributes. The acronym stands for:

Command

Leverage

Expectations

Audience

Relationship

Listening

Inspiration

In our next chapter, we will address three core frameworks that we use with clients at Change Masters. In the subsequent chapters, we will describe each of our CLEARLI Authentic Executive Presence attributes and how you can increase your efficacy in each one.

This book captures many of the perspectives and approaches that we have found most effective over two decades of leadership communications coaching with many talented businesspeople. Many of them have found these insights to be life-changing. Our hope is that you will, too.

Here is a brief description of our seven CLEARLI Authentic Executive Presence attributes.

COMMAND of the Room with Charisma

Some people own their space, projecting ease, warmth and capability. People observe your walk, posture, facial expression, vocal impact and dress quality to assess executive presence. They watch how you enter a room, sit in a chair and graciously interact with others. Command of the room with gracious charisma is the look and sound of confidence, conviction and competence based on non-verbal behavior.

LEVERAGE Influence and Power

Achieving great results requires knowing how to influence others and also understanding the organization's power and politics. The most influential leaders use influence without being seen as political. They know how to use the power they've been given in a values-based manner. Being an effective influencer with authentic political savvy is not an oxymoron. It's achievable and essential to your success.

EXPECTATIONS: Strategic and Tactical

Executive presence means you can move back and forth easily between strategic vision and tactical direction. Both need to be articulated well and connected continuously. Creating an engaging vision for a goal or project gives the tasks meaning. Execution makes a strategic vision more real and relevant. Mastery of both allows you to create and capture value. We present ideas to help you keep people on track using our expectation-setting model.

AUDIENCE Connections

Presentations have changed the trajectory of many high-level careers. Connecting with the audience is what makes the difference. Outstanding presentation skills can dramatically impact the direction and commitment of an organization. Formal and informal presentations of information are the moments in which people significantly assess your capability. Even small-group presentations in front of the right audience can be pivotal. Maximizing your presentations with these tips will dramatically increase your memorable executive presence.

RELATIONSHIP Competence Locally and Remotely

Interpersonal skills have always been key to leadership success. Their importance has been increased by globalization, diversity, instantaneous communications and the expectation of 24/7 electronic interactions. The speed and access of communications has changed how we lead around the world, in different buildings or across the table. We are all dependent on so many people to get our jobs done today. Managing relationships well can make or break your effectiveness both locally and around the globe.

LISTENING Engagement

Most executives think they are much better listeners than others do. Great listening is not just great hearing. The test of a good listener is whether the other person feels heard and understood. Several studies have identified listening as the most critical success factor for executives. You spend over half your day listening to others; you may as well get good at it!

INSPIRATION, Motivation and Praise

Praise and motivation matter. If you're not consistently reinforcing what you expect, you won't get what you expect. People deliver best when they feel valued and respected, no matter what pressures exist. To get the biggest impact for the praise you deliver, demonstrate honest warmth with engaged poise, because praise from you matters more than you know.

We have worked for two decades with clientele who have diverse backgrounds including nationality, race, gender, sexual orientation, values, religion and age. The CLEARLI executive presence attributes have applied to all of them. They have found great benefit in learning these attributes to be more effective in their workplaces while still being able to be true to themselves.

Aligning Internal and External Authenticity

So often, well-intentioned leaders are misunderstood because their internal and external authenticity are not aligned. It is not enough to have good intentions. You need to also make sure others understand your intentions and context so you get credit for your efforts. Juan, a senior executive we worked with, learned the importance of communicating context in a very measurable way.

Juan had received feedback from the annual employee survey that his team didn't feel he was paying enough attention to their personal development plans. So Juan made an earnest, concerted effort to actively help his people improve their skills over the course of the next twelve months. Unfortunately, the next annual employee survey showed no measurable change in the employees' assessment of his interest in their personal development.

Juan was understandably feeling frustrated and unappreciated. He had spent so much time trying to help his team grow and yet he was getting no recognition for it. He wondered what they wanted from him. He was grousing about this to a peer at lunch one day. She looked at him with a smile and wisely counseled him, "Juan, it's obvious to you what you're trying to do, but clearly it's not obvious to them. Why don't you just start out each development conversation by telling them what you're doing?"

It seemed too simple, but it made sense. For the next year Juan routinely started each conversation about personal development by saying, "I'm interested in your personal development and that's what I would like to talk about today." That was the only thing he changed for the year. To Juan's amazement, the survey results for year two showed dramatic improvement in his perceived commitment to employee development across the board.

For his people to understand his internal authentic interest in their personal development, Juan needed to effectively communicate his context and intent so others could see the external manifestations of his deep commitment to and interest in them. Often the biggest opportunities are simple once you see yourself as others do.

As the Chinese philosopher Confucius said, "When it is obvious that the goals cannot be reached, don't adjust the goals—adjust your actions."

The diagram below summarizes the book. At the bottom are the foundations for executive presence. The seven C.L.E.A.R.L.I. authentic executive presence attributes build on the foundations.

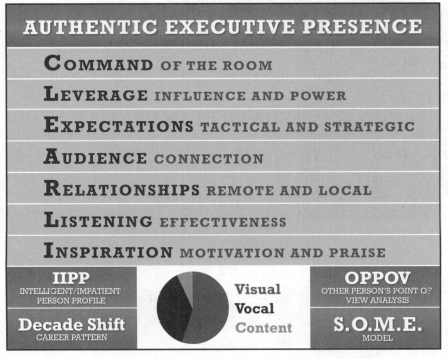

The next chapter provides the foundations for executive presence.

C OMMAND

L EVERAGE

E XPECTATIONS

A UDIENCE

R ELATIONSHIP

L ISTENING

I NSPIRATION

2

COMMUNICATION
FOUNDATIONS

There are three concepts we use with Change Masters' clients because of their universal applicability. These foundational skills reliably help our clients more readily understand others, themselves and the situations they face. They cross all seven CLEARLI executive presence attributes. They are the Decade Shift, the Intelligent Impatient Person Profile and the Other Person's Point Of View analysis. All these concepts rest upon our specialty area, leadership communications—the effective correlation of visual, vocal and content messages to communicate what you really mean.

The Decade Shift profile helps you understand the typical communication maturation progression for yourself and others. The Intelligent Impatient Person Profile provides valuable insights whether you fit this communication pattern or deal with someone who does. The Other Person's Point of View (OPPOV) is a quick and powerful analysis tool to determine the best way to interact with those around you.

Foundation Skill One: Decade Shift Profile

We found there are universal expectations in your career that are based on the decade you're in at the time. These expectations are seldom articulated to us and yet we are judged on them all the time. After analyzing ten years of Change Masters' client surveys and research on their experiences, we developed our "Decade Shift" profile to describe the unspoken expectations that change during your career. Without awareness, these expectations can impact how you're perceived. They can help you or become an impediment to your success. The Decade Shift profile gives you a road map with insights to get you ahead of the race by illustrating patterns that apply across most industries and companies.

> **The same behaviors we accept from a 25-year-old we won't accept from someone who is 35 or 45 years old.**

The same behaviors we accept from a 25-year-old we won't accept from someone who is 35 or 45 years old. The characteristics you may have been rewarded for early in your career can easily become obstacles later. If your behaviors are not what others expect and you don't realize how people see you, it will impact your perceived authenticity, your effectiveness and your personal satisfaction with your job. When your skills are not developed as expected, your career can plateau prematurely.

Chronological age is no guarantee of maturity. There are some 25-year-olds who are more mature than certain 52-year-olds, but generally speaking, people do become more mature as they age. They may just have blind spots where they're missing some expectations others have of them today. Roughly every decade in our clients' careers there was a significant change in the characteristics companies wanted to see from them. Expectations changed, but no one told them. They just knew that some of the things that had created their earlier success were no longer as successful.

John was a client from a financial services company who was deeply impacted by the Decade Shift concept. He told us, "I used to think that when things got wacky in my work life, I should just work harder—it wasn't out of valor, it was about coping. It allowed me to wrap my brain around something I could control instead of something I couldn't. Just because other people didn't want to work as hard as I did was their problem, not mine. As long as I got things done, I didn't have to care about how I interacted with anyone.

"But one day working harder wasn't enough. It's scary when you keep pushing the buttons that have worked in the past and nothing happens like it used to. I needed to learn a new way of dealing with the world, to collaborate and lead people instead of just pumping out more data at them."

As John learned, over the course of your career, the overall focus of the Decade Shift profile represents a shift from task orientation to a relationship orientation. The further you advance in your career, the less "hands on" you are, so your relationship skills are what keep you achieving as you move ahead. In the first two decades of your career, results alone can make you successful. The last two decades are about coupling results with leading people to get things done.

The Decade Shift profile also helps you realize how your maturity level stacks up to that of your peers at any given stage in your career. Those on the leadership fast track need to move even faster through the Decade Shift profile. For example, a 35-year-old just promoted to senior level needs to display the behaviors of someone well into their 40s.

Here is a partial breakout of each decade:

The 20s

In your 20s, it's all about making your mark through task completion, which allows you to be a great individual producer. We've all known people who get stuck in a task orientation mindset that lasts late into their careers. They were probably recognized for how well they did tasks in their 20s, so they have a hard time letting go of that reward decades later.

If you "break a little glass" or step on a few toes in your early 20s, it's tolerated much more than at any other point in your career. People know you're still young and learning. A little more independence and a little less adherence to norms is tolerated at this stage. Because you're primarily getting things done through your own efforts and intensity rather than through others, you can afford to be more narcissistic. Don't get too comfortable with this view, however, because the expectations around individualized contributions versus team play will change dramatically in the next decade.

Most of your peers are still pretty focused on themselves rather than having the perspective of how they're impacting the larger organization. You can stand out from the crowd quickly with just a little more awareness and better choices on how you're being seen by others.

In this decade you learn how to navigate the cultural and political waters you're suddenly dealing with after a more free-form college existence. Now you're simultaneously handling multiple projects on a team rather than just having a couple of term papers due here and there. You move from learning the ropes of how to work in a professional setting early on in the decade. But by the middle or end of the decade you are expected to take on more responsibility. It's a lot to take in—maybe it should be called a "quarter-life crisis" because it's so similar to the mid-life crisis people can have in their 40s! If you can show a solid work ethic, have clear priorities, knowledge of the industry and an interpersonal awareness skill set in your 20s, you will set an early trajectory for your success providing a significant head start over your peers.

The 30s

In your 30s you're expected to collaborate. You have to develop the ability to enlist the support of others rather than doing it all alone. There is a growing recognition that your job is getting bigger and you can't do it all yourself. Your choices at this point can lead to some missteps or set the stage for accelerated career growth.

Influencing cross-functional change, speaking up early and with confidence are beginning to become much more important at this time. In addition to collaboration, self-discipline, motivational skills, conflict-management skills and goal orientation are expected in your 30s. Effective team leadership to get things done through others is the key skill to master in this decade. It's a very big shift in skills and life experience from 30 to 39. You may be shifting into life balance issues with your new family or may be deciding to go back to school to get an MBA.

Impulse control is expected from you now despite the huge demands of your job. If you feel stressed at this stage, you're not alone. It's becoming too much to try to get it all done every day, so you need to prioritize more effectively than ever before. Prior to joining Change Masters, Carol Keers worked in the field of executive outplacement, where she found that the early seeds of discontent or future termination were sown for many people around age 37 or 38. For many at this stage, there is an uneasy feeling that what got you here won't keep you here. This is the time when you realize that doing the same things that used to work in your 20s suddenly don't get the same results. Learning new skills to counter this plateauing can change this decade from being daunting to an exciting growth decade, personally and professionally.

The 40s

The years of the early 40s are perhaps the most pivotal point in your career trajectory, because they determine where you'll end up years later. One of our sponsors said, "It's a crossroad period of a career—at this level, the skill set I look for is judgment, the realization that there is no perfect solution, and the ability to craft a vision and align people behind it. If you have too much project-orientation at this stage, you lean toward knocking off the tasks because that's in your comfort zone. You have to learn to influence rather than control, since it's too big for you to control anymore."

It all depends on the choices you make. You can break out or burn out in your 40s. You've hit the half-way mark in your career, a time when many wonder, "Is this all there is?" It's a long way to retirement, so how do you revive your energy? Your 40s can be a time of metamorphosis that will propel you through the last half of your career or a mid-life crisis that can stall you out.

The promotion pyramid around you is getting narrower and narrower. Not only are there fewer opportunities for advancement than there were before, when you routinely moved up with more responsibility, there's more competition than ever. All around you are talented peers who have just as much technical competence as you do. You are expected to work smoothly and effectively across disciplines. More extensive strategic perspective is expected from you since you're not just in a tactical role any more. In order to differentiate yourself to be seen as a broader thought leader, the question becomes, "So what else have you got?" These distinctive differences are your ability to influence people and communicate vision to "get the geese to fly in the same direction." The "what else can you offer" isn't about your technical skills. It's assumed you are technically competent, so the differentiator is primarily communication- and relationship-based.

You are now the person your employees talk about at the dinner table.

Selling your teams' efforts as well as your own is more crucial than ever before. Your work no longer speaks for itself. No one is looking out for you in the same way they did before, so you need to take the initiative to promote achievement in an authentic, engaged manner.

It is also likely you will receive less praise even when you are doing well. Do not let this distract you or allow it to create resentment. At this point, you need to give much more praise than you receive.

Since you're far less hands-on than you used to be, it is critical that you get others to tell you bad news early enough to take action. That requires emotional competence in order to build trust, since most of the results you're measured on today are being achieved through others. Building strong successors becomes important.

You are admired—or feared—because you have more impact than you realize. Others watch you to learn the fate of the firm. You are now the person your employees talk about at the dinner table.

The 50s and Beyond

This is the period of harvesting the hard work you've done for the last several decades. In your 50s and 60s seasoned leadership is displayed by moving large groups to successful outcomes with value-based integrity and wisdom gained through impeccable listening. All of these things help you build your legacy. A big-picture, strategic view is necessary since you're now the orchestra conductor looking at the musical score for all the musicians.

If you don't realize your impact on those below you in this decade, you will fail to maximize the investment of the previous 30 or 40 years you've put in, because you now have a major ripple effect on people. They look to you for guidance and comfort in difficult times. Your praise will impact others more than you know. A single smile—or frown—from you in the hallway can impact hundreds of people, directly or indirectly.

Granted, some people have plateaued and are just going through the motions without making waves, waiting for the day they can retire. We don't work with those people. For our clients this period is marked by astute, sage, shrewd judgment and the perspective to see things in a broader strategic light based on years of experience.

You can glean great satisfaction in your role by using your hard-acquired wisdom to grow others and you can share it by dedicating a part of your day to connect with and mentor others. It is a valid, necessary part of your job to reach out and help the subsequent generations to support the legacy you've built in the final act of your career. Most leaders have no idea how much it will mean to a talented younger employee when they recognize and groom their talents. It will cast you in their memory as an esteemed leader. As a client told us, "I'd rather have them regret that I'm going instead of rejoicing!"

Foundation Skill Two:
The Intelligent Impatient Person Profile

Intensity plus power equals intimidation. The intensity that is honored when we're younger can critically impact us when we're older because we have so much more power. Some people intimidate others on purpose, but most people who have received this feedback have no idea why people tell them they're intimidating.

Change Masters' Intelligent Impatient Person Profile (IIPP) explains this confusion. We created our IIPP after working with hundreds of incredibly bright people. We found a consistent pattern of behaviors. People who had been reinforced for their IQ earlier in their education and careers had to learn it can be a liability later in life if overused. You only need enough intelligence to do the job, but not so much that it gets in the way. You do not need to act dumb, but you do need to be thoughtful in how you communicate.

I realized that IQ is not the currency at this stage as it was earlier in my career.

One of our IIPP clients from Mattel said, "I realized that IQ is not the currency at this stage as it was when I was earlier in my career. I don't try to impress people with how smart I am anymore, because the currency today is how well you deal with relationships. That greases the wheels and makes connections so others can hear what you bring to the table."

Intensity, intelligence and intimidation are often conjoined in our very bright and accomplished clientele. An example of this was a client we'll call Joseph, from Procter and Gamble. Joseph managed groups of people in North and South America. He realized his intensity and intimidation capability when he saw himself on camera. Joseph said, "I just didn't know that when I barreled down the hall with the people back in Cincinnati (P&G's corporate headquarters) and made no eye contact with them, they assumed I was angry! I wasn't angry at them—I was just trying to get to my next meeting on time! One of my people who was in an off-site location had the courage to tell me that when my name came up on his phone or e-mail, he felt an anxious feeling in his stomach. That just shattered me because it wasn't what I meant to do to such a great employee.

"I immediately saw when you put me on camera how I was negatively impacting relationships, because I didn't realize how angry I could appear with my content and my non-verbal patterns. My intensity, something I'd always thought was such a good thing, looked pissed off! When I was upset, it was even worse. I have to change my patterns or I'm going to lose my team's support."

Well, not only did Joseph change his patterns, he ultimately ended up getting a major promotion based on his people skills. Joseph has a 15-year runway left before he retires, so you can only imagine how these realizations about his intimidation and intensity will increase his effectiveness.

What really describes Joseph's blind spot of intensity is Change Masters' Intelligent Impatient Person Profile. Your intelligence can rapidly make you too impatient. If you're too focused and intense you miss those subtle cues and nuances that create connection and authenticity, both at work and at home.

If you're younger or are an individual producer who's working alone, you can go as fast as you want most of the time, but in a leadership role you have to pace things differently or you'll lose the people around you. The fast-moving brains of people demonstrating this pattern can work against showing gracious presence and they have no idea it's happening.

Behaviors of the Intelligent Impatient Person

Examples of behaviors we see in the Intelligent Impatient Person Profile are:

- Loving to debate—and being extremely good at it!
- Deciding they know what the other person is saying before they finish
- Observing the world ironically or cynically
- Highly competitive
- Very street smart
- Very intense and driven
- Having poor listening skills, interrupting, multi-tasking
- "Yes, but"-ers

What's a "Yes, but"-er? Someone who opens every reaction to what they hear with the phrase, "Yes, but..." and then goes into a detailed debate of your idea. One of our clients, a lawyer by training, instantly recognized this pattern in herself on tape and declared, "I owe my son an apology." When asked why, she said, "I've been nailing him for always saying, 'Yeah, but Mom...' and now I can see just where he gets it!"

If this pattern describes you

How can you shift this Intelligent Impatient Person Profile if it applies to you? Try these three things:

1. Warm up and slow down your communication style in terms of vocal and visual delivery.
2. Simplify your content—choose one line of thinking, not three!
3. Take a few more minutes up front to connect, listen and understand.

It is not realistic to slow down 100% of the time for someone who fits the IIPP. It is realistic to purposely slow down when it counts the most. A total shift in approach that's typically needed toward more overt demonstration of warmth and connection is less than 25% of the time.

One of our clients, a Division President, thought we'd written the IIPP just for him. It turned out to be a key accelerator of perceived maturity through his Change Masters coaching. He told us, "The hardest thing you could have asked me a year ago when I started with Change Masters was to describe how I felt, because I was so out of touch with that part of myself at work and at home. I now can safely say I have much more emotional self-confidence.

"Outwardly today, I am more calm and measured. I went from being an incredibly intense person who was only focused on production to showing mature executive presence. Inwardly, I've become a much more confident individual since I'm more self-aware than ever before. The development of emotional intelligence resulting in self-confidence really surprised me. I've started to have more of a people emphasis—more direct feedback, bonding with the team and less emphasis on process.

"It's ironic—awareness of my intensity has given me tremendous confidence to be more sensitive to the nuances people are showing me all the time. It was a life-changing experience for me."

If this pattern describes someone you need to influence

Conversely, to more effectively influence someone who has the IIPP pattern:

1. Keep your content concise and crisp.
2. Make your message relevant—start with the payoff to them and then link that payoff to what interests them.
3. Be engaging in the delivery or you'll lose them.

> It's ironic—awareness of my intensity has given me tremendous confidence to be more sensitive to the nuances people are showing me all the time. It was a life-changing experience for me.

Annette, one of our European clients, who had been raised to be overly respectful of hierarchy, told us that what she learned about how to deal with people fitting the IIPP profile, "Intense people can be intimidating to challenge, but once you realize you have to be clear, relevant and hold your ground with them in order to be respected and heard, you can finally get on their radar screen. There's lots of helpful information these people are giving you on how to deal with them all the time—if you know how to pay attention and adjust your style."

V V C—The Total Communication Message

Intensity is only one of the filters people use to interpret the total communication message. Communication from the receiver's perspective is a combination of visual, vocal and content. Most of us think of our content as the message. We know our intent, but we do not fully understand how we communicate visually and vocally.

Malcolm Gladwell noted this concept of "thin-slicing" in his book *Blink: The Power Of Thinking Without Thinking*. Thin-slicing describes the momentary assessments people form about others in a matter of seconds, even with people they know well.

Albert Mehrabian's landmark studies on non-verbal communications align with Gladwell's concepts. They showed that only 7 percent of that initial impact is content-based. People start to form assessments of others rapidly—in less than seven seconds—even with people we know well. This is not just the first time we meet someone. It is when we walk into a meeting or arrive home from work and interact with our family.

According to Mehrabian, the breakout of the characteristics that create initial perception are:

55% visual attributes

38% vocal quality factors

7% content

This means that 93% of the initial impression being made is non-verbal, even with familiar contacts. These figures do change during the course of the conversation, but even over time, non-verbal factors are nearly half of how you're perceived. That's a lot to leave to the unknown.

To enhance your ability to be effective as both a communicator and leader it is important to consider the way in which you are perceived by others and determine how those perceptions impact your effectiveness. With this understanding you can begin to make more effective choices in your communication approaches and behaviors.

What Do You Believe?

When there is a disconnect between the visual indicators, vocal cues and content in the messages you send, your ability to influence the room diminishes significantly.

For example, let's say you ask your boss how he's doing as he walks into the office. He responds "Great. Just great," but has a frown, a gruff voice and no eye contact as he trudges into his office and slams his briefcase down with a bang.

What do you really believe? Certainly not his words. The visual and vocal messages are saying much more that's credible to you than his content. When this type of inconsistency exists, we typically believe the visual and vocal over the words that are said.

This is because when we are listening to someone we have a meter in our heads that says either:

- I believe what they are saying
- I don't believe them

Unconsciously, we look at the visual, vocal and content communications to see if they are aligned. If they are aligned, we tend to believe they are telling the truth and are being authentic. But if the visual and vocal communications say something different from the content, people don't believe it.

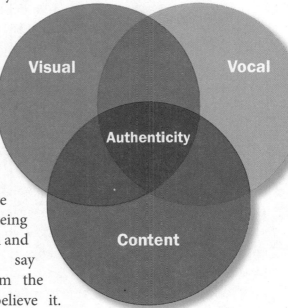

Author Susanne Elgin puts it this way: "No words cancel body language. Any words, be they ever so flawless, can have their meaning cancelled by body language."

When you link all three factors in a total communication package to say the same thing at the same time, you are perceived to be credible and authentic in your communications.

Foundation Skill Three: OPPOV™

The Power of Understanding the Other Person's Point Of View

We're asked often what interferes most with effective communication. That's easy—it's ignoring the other person's point of view. This error causes people to get so stuck in their views of the world; they can't see any other perspectives as being viable.

> We've seen OPPOV™ dramatically affect how successfully clients are able to influence and persuade others.

Being stuck in your point of view can range from benign neglect—people saying, "Well, I just never thought of it that way," to a deliberate, stubborn refusal to consider the input of a specific person. One banking executive initially told us, only half facetiously, "You mean other people have a point of view?"

To help our clients be more facile in looking at others' perspectives, we created a tool called OPPOV, or the Other Person's Point Of View. As leadership situations become more complex and ambiguous, OPPOV can help people consider, deal with and incorporate multiple perspectives simultaneously. This audience analysis tool involves evaluating how another person sees his or her world and experiences you. It's a quick and accurate approach that helps you see many new and different angles to broaden your point of view. We've seen OPPOV dramatically affect how successfully clients are able to influence and persuade others.

There are five questions of OPPOV, three about others and two about you.

1. What are they rewarded for?

What does anyone in this role get paid to do? (e.g., revenue generation, smooth operations, customer satisfaction, on-time delivery, increasing stock price)

2. What are they motivated by?

What do they personally seem to like or need? What moves them, either intrinsically or extrinsically? (e.g., ego, control, power, being liked, making a contribution, free time to do other things, family time, recognition from above, expensive toys, creating a legacy)

3. What are they afraid of?

What scares them—what do they not want to happen? (e.g., looking foolish, surprises, not having the answer, loss of their job, being left out of the decision process, not being liked, loss of respect, public image or their spouse's expectations.) People don't always broadcast their concerns to you, so the quick version of this is to reverse the rewards and motivations. Once you do, you'll understand their fears.

4. What am I doing to make things worse?

Be honest. What have you done that's negatively impacting what they're rewarded for or motivated by? What might you be doing that could be tapping into their fears?

5. What could I do to make things better?

Knowing this, what specific behaviors could you do that would make a difference? Taking accountability for starting positive change in any significant work or personal relationship will make you the bigger person. No matter what your age, it will demonstrate your authentic, mature executive presence.

The OPPOV questions allow you to develop your tactical approach toward relationship awareness.

S.O.M.E. Adaptations to Communication

To look at your communication from an even broader perspective, use the strategy of the S.O.M.E. adaptations approach, which incorporates the OPPOV analysis into an assessment of how to handle all aspects of a challenging communication situation.

We created the concept of S.O.M.E. from the fact that when changing your approach to communications, you never have to alter everything all at once; you just need to make some adaptations. The goal of using the S.O.M.E. adaptations approach is to have increased awareness on how you impact others to manage the communication situations you face more effectively. The payoff of using this technique is increased awareness from moment to moment to show executive presence.

Developing the S.O.M.E. Adaptations Approach

Assess your communications according to the following criteria:

S. = Situation

What's going on, who is here, what objectively needs to happen in this interaction?

O. = OPPOV

What is the Other Person's Point Of View?

M. = My Point Of View

What do you believe should happen? How do you see the situation?

E. = Expression

How do you adapt your visual, vocal, and content messages to be more effective and appropriate for this situation?

Here's an example of how one of our clients used the S.O.M.E. approach to take a fresh look at a challenging situation he faced:

Situation

The Operating Committee needs to reach mutually agreeable solutions on some sticky issues that impact each of them in unique ways and will greatly impact their fiscal year. They are going to be meeting with the CEO.

OPPOV = they are:

rewarded for: having the best results of the group, getting their ideas accepted in this platform

motivated by: competitiveness, their peers buying into their point of view; acceptance by the CEO

afraid of: losing face with the CEO; losing turf or funding

MPOV

I need to challenge their ideas in a way they can hear instead of swallowing my frustration, lashing out or making them look bad in front of the CEO. I want the group to see the situation in a completely new light and not get stuck in old ruts.

Expression

I need to use a calmer, more seasoned voice and body language. It's important to show more engaged listening, reinforce my peers where appropriate and show them how these ideas could be adopted to help them grow throughout the meeting. Be patient! Don't check out if I think I know where they're going! I need to help the Operating Committee use a more unified approach to solving this issue through the questions I ask. I have to get my point of view out sooner and in a more compelling manner so the CEO can get a sense for what I'm doing that's working.

Retroactive Analysis

In addition to using the S.O.M.E. adaptations approach to plan communications, you can use the OPPOV to quickly do a retroactive analysis on a situation that didn't go well. It can help you figure out what to do differently in the future.

Skilled users of OPPOV can do it in the hallway while walking to a meeting. In return, you receive tremendous gain in your ability to objectively see situations as others do and display executive presence in challenging or persuasion situations.

Using the Foundation Framework and Skills

Decade Shifts, the Intelligent Impatient Person Profile and Other Person's Point Of View with the S.O.M.E. analysis all create a solid foundation for workplace communication.

These simple and pragmatic tools are the foundation used in the seven Authentic Executive Presence Attributes. We have seen the impact of these tools on our clients over more than twenty-five years and we know that even the simplest changes can have profound impact if they are the right changes. To help you get to where you want to go, the rest of this book will expand on the seven CLEARLI Authentic Executive Presence attributes.

C OMMAND

L EVERAGE

E XPECTATIONS

A UDIENCE

R ELATIONSHIP

L ISTENING

I NSPIRATION

3

COMMAND OF THE ROOM WITH CHARISMA

The first attribute of executive presence is how you command the room. Some people project ease, competence and courage. They appear to own their space, no matter what the situation requires. They have captured a sense of authentic confidence and charisma to command the room.

We all know what confidence looks like, but charisma is far more elusive for people. Some believe you have to be born with charisma or you will never have it. We don't. We've seen too many legendary leaders who have intentionally developed charisma in a credible manner. Winston Churchill, John Kennedy and James Earl Jones, people who became charismatic and confident communicators, were all awkward, shy children.

You can command the room without charisma, if you demonstrate confidence. However, if you are cold and arrogant you run a much higher risk of people turning on you when problems emerge. When you couple confidence and charisma, you create a memorable legacy of leadership, in good times and bad.

We're not here to tell you how to gain confidence internally. That is a tremendously personal journey. We can tell you, however, how to authentically show what we've found to be effective approaches to increase perceived confidence and charisma.

Charisma is Not a Gift

Charisma is not a gift given just to a select few who have the gift of gab or an innate love of people. Sixty percent of all CEOs are introverts. They're not comfortable in the public-facing activities. But those who do it well had to learn how to demonstrate charisma when it counts, whether they like doing the highly visible functions or not.

Commanding the room through gracious charisma allows you to inspire a group you lead by the power of your presence, no matter what is happening around you. Our most memorable leaders are engaging, authentic and powerful at the same time.

Like ice cream, charisma comes in many flavors. There's no one way to show it. Some who have it are cool and aloof with just a hint of charm and others are warm and engaging. You can't have executive presence just based on your charisma, but it is a key component of the total executive presence package.

The Likeability Factor

Blending kindness with capability makes you really stand out. For many of us in this stressed-out workplace, charisma and command of the room can be enhanced greatly by increased likeability. Sometimes you have to appear likeable even if you don't feel like it that day.

Roger Ailes, author of *You Are the Message—Getting What You Want by Being Who You Are,* stresses the concept of "likeability." Ailes calls likeability "the magic bullet" in authentic leadership presence and charisma. He says, "If people like you, they'll forgive you for just about anything, but if they don't like you, you can do everything right, and it won't matter." Someone who learned this was Jonathan.

Jonathan was an intense, sarcastic Group Vice President in a medical technology firm who learned the wisdom of likeability in his coaching work with us. When we completed our coaching process, he said:

"I never realized likeability was so important when interacting with people. Before, it was just a job to me. Who knew you needed to be pleasant to people? I thought I was a decent person, but the person I saw on tape was so condescending. Once I stopped knocking people, I found out I had a sense of humor after all and it made such a difference in how I am seen. I'm much more relaxed now. I found out it's OK to be more of who I am, not less. I'm almost relieved to find this out because I was really getting burned out. I was on a road of self-destruction. I had tried throughout my career not to be seen as weak. It was exhausting, it annoyed others and it didn't work. Thank you for helping me see how I can be more of myself."

Jonathan grew tremendously in the eyes of his organization based on this realization—and gained enormous productivity by not exhausting others!

Charismatic Enough

How one commands the room and displays charisma depends on subtle, controllable behaviors. Consciously or unconsciously, how you look when you walk into a room, how you sound when you greet others, the way you clearly express your thoughts or hold eye contact determine how you are perceived.

People become caught up in the energy of a charismatic person. Charisma is the magnetism that enables you to significantly influence and engage others. You've seen it—you've felt it from certain special people who you've been lucky enough to encounter in your life. Have you ever forgotten them? We all know people who have been treated charmingly or graciously by a celebrity, an executive, or a politician and talk about it for the rest of their lives. They remember each second of that encounter. You have a chance to have a similar impact. OK, so maybe you'll never be Bill Clinton or Ronald Reagan, people who are often identified to us as those who have demonstrated charisma and executive presence. But the reality is you have a lot more ability to demonstrate command of the room than you think. With insights and guidance, you can effectively reach out to others and show a level of engagement that draws people toward you.

Most people feel they'll never be charismatic enough. They compare themselves to bigger-than-life icons, so the standard seems unachievable and overwhelming. In reality, as the leader of one of our clients said, "I don't need her to be Oprah Winfrey. I just need her to be more welcoming, for people to jump on board with her more readily because she's exuding confidence with a positive, upbeat attitude." When our client realized the criteria for success, charisma and command of the room became an achievable goal.

The Power of Genuine Charisma

One example of powerful charisma was an extremely wealthy business owner we worked with many, many years ago. He could be charming. He also could be explosive under pressure, even abusive in the eyes of some of his people. Paradoxically, his goal was to achieve increased productivity. Studies show that one blow-up every six months decreases leadership effectiveness and productivity by up to 50 percent, since people are tiptoeing around, just waiting for the next explosion.

No one was forcing this man to get coaching. He owned the company. Nevertheless, something drove this financially successful man to figure out why he treated so badly the people he cared about so deeply. When he saw himself on tape and read the feedback from the team he was so committed to, he wept. With characteristic determination, he decided to recalibrate his life on many different levels, because his perceptions were so out of line with his value system. He was so successful, he literally transformed his life.

We spoke to him five years after our original session and he was a much happier person, at peace with himself while still having fun. He told us, "Change Masters' coaching is like having a personal trainer for your interpersonal skill set and emotional competence. This knowledge is cumulative and transferable. I've learned to coach and guide my people on a whole different level."

Showing Confidence

It is the rare individual who is confident and capable in all situations from the very outset of their career. Most of us have had to learn to act as if we were capable and confident in a wide variety of tense situations, because we are never completely ready for our next big stretch job.

"Act as if" is a phrase borrowed from twelve-step recovery programs. In our context, it means that you often have to demonstrate composure even when you are shaky inside. You may not have the experience to feel confident in what you're doing, yet you still need to portray confidence with others to obtain their buy-in.

This concept has been demonstrated repeatedly on Confidence Lab, a BBC reality TV program. On the show, people who lack confidence reinvent themselves over the course of just one week. The themes that show up repeatedly are the importance of making good first impressions; great posture; having positive, fifteen-second "commercials" about themselves and asking open-ended questions for conversation starters. It is not a superficial exercise. Repeatedly, Confidence Lab graduates have maintained their newfound strength, received promotions and landed prestigious new jobs.

Psychologist Ros Taylor, primary consultant for the show, says, "Psychologically, action precedes change. If you start doing things in a more confident fashion, it feeds back to your brain that you might actually BE confident. All of these people [on the show] went through profound cognitive shifts about what they could do." Leaders with charisma and executive presence routinely step outside their comfort zones to influence and affect those around them—no matter what they feel inside. This is critical to remember because most of us live in comfort zones that are three sizes too small! To expand your comfort zone you need to move out of it, so you will feel uncomfortable initially. The truth is that you have to "fake it 'til you make it" at times. By expanding your range, one day, you'll realize you're no longer faking it—you've authentically mastered a significantly larger comfort zone.

One way to act confidently when you're under pressure is to think of role models to emulate physically and vocally. Putting yourself in their shoes helps to show the poise you may not yet possess.

We ask our seminar and individual clients to think of someone they know who lacks confidence, presence or warmth and list all the non-verbal behaviors this person displays. Then they select someone they respect who demonstrates executive presence, high confidence, warmth or enthusiasm. We have them note in detail what behaviors make this person seem so powerful and engaging.

To complete this exercise, we ask one person to act like the person they have chosen who lacks confidence. Next, we have them act like the person they identified who displays power, presence and impact. We coach them to demonstrate the nuances of how these individuals walk, talk and look at others. They practice the gestures, content and poise of those they respect.

It is fascinating to see what a difference they are able to achieve through subtle nuances and still be authentic. Building this awareness allows our seminar participants and individual clients to understand what is needed to show the exterior authenticity and executive presence they so respect in others.

Ways to Display Command of the Room

Most of our initial perceived command of the room comes from what we show the world non-verbally. It's a balance of openness and determined commitment, healthy humility and belief in oneself. We've identified the following four exterior behaviors that, when linked with authentic internal choices, make the most impact for our clients:

1. Visual impact
2. Vocal impact
3. Clear, compelling content choices
4. Managing physical stress under pressure

As Dr. Maya Angelou, professor, poet and author says in her book *Wouldn't Take Nothing for My Journey Now*:

"Content is of great importance, but we must not underrate the value of style. Attention must be paid to not only what is said, but how it is said."

It only takes a moment to make an impact. As noted in the last chapter, 93 percent of what influences the way an interaction will unfold is determined in the first few seconds, and is almost exclusively based on non-content cues.

> **Most of our initial perceived command of the room comes from what we show the world non-verbally.**

We tend to think of our own communications in terms of just our content, but others are reacting to much more than our content all the time. The first factor of command of the room is visual impact.

Visual Impact

Osmo Vänskä, the highly charismatic conductor of the Minnesota Orchestra, said if he isn't showing confidence on the podium, the musicians get tense and the music sounds as nervous as they feel. When you link the three visual, vocal and content factors of communication, you create a sense of confidence, trust and power for the orchestra you're leading.

The first aspect of commanding the room to register with people is the visual component. Those who project a compelling look may have a "warm" or "cool" command of the room, yet they seem to be confident, no matter what they're doing or what's going on. They are fully in the moment. You may not have their attention for very long, but when you're with them, you're the only one in their world. Their non-verbal messages help create that perception of connection.

Others notice whether you're stressed or relaxed and they respond accordingly. When the tension builds, people evaluate every nuance for cues. As one of our clients said, "I understand now that when I walk, people are watching. I'm learning to walk with the ease I have when I'm on vacation, but just a bit faster!"

Fill Your Space

In our society, confidence is demonstrated by holding—holding the gesture calmly, holding the eye contact and holding the stance. Be calm below your waist and engaged above with engaged facial expression and strong gestures. Anchor your feet and squeeze your toes to direct your nervous energy downward. This works invisibly to ground the movement that would otherwise make you look uncomfortable. Shrinking, perching or tensing up awkwardly in your chair does not look confident. When you fill the whole space you occupy you look more confident. Fill your space with wider, slower hand and head movements instead of smaller, more rapid ones. To show charisma, competence and confidence, your physical movements need to be bigger and smoother. When you make them jerky, short, and fast, you lose the potential to command the room authentically. Be more like a lion than a deer. A deer is nervously scanning the environment at all times. A lion lying in the sun is relaxed and deliberate, but it can run 35 miles an hour if needed. To emulate the lion, sit all the way back in your chair or if you're standing, put your feet shoulder-width apart. Put some air in your armpits to fill your space by using wider, slower gestures than you normally do to emphasize points and maintain steady, even eye contact. This will allow your body to tell your brain that you are in control.

Managing Facial Expressions

Your earliest communication skill was to read facial expressions. Infants are experts at reading non-verbal cues. They spend their days scanning faces and listening to voices. None of us has lost the non-verbal expertise we once had—we've just layered language over the top of it!

Your expression flickers by before you know it, but others have already seen and registered it. Your face is like a TV screen, so it's important to become aware of what program your face is broadcasting because others are always watching and interpreting you. As a result, most people are subconsciously very perceptive about nonverbal expression. It takes a half-second to change your facial expression, but only 1/25th of a second for someone else to interpret it. Just 1/16th of an inch movement on your face can be detected as a change in your facial expression. The interpretation of facial expressions varies internationally. In the United States, pulling up the corners of the eyes, the brow and the mouth is seen as positive. Tightening or flattening those same facial features is seen as critical.

Psychologist Paul Eckman is an expert on interpreting facial expressions. He says that while facial expressions can be hard to decipher because they're so rapid, they are the clearest indicator of what someone is feeling. That's because each emotion has unique, identifiable facial patterns, which he has painstakingly categorized. Emotions manifest themselves in facial expressions because, says Eckman, it was evolutionarily useful to let others know when we sensed danger and facial expressions were the only silent way to do so. How does that relate to your workplace?

Meredith Levinson echoed this concept when she wrote in *CIO* magazine, "Reading facial expression is a particularly useful skill for business executives because so often in business settings, people don't say what they really think. When the CIO is able to be aware by visually recognizing different emotions, they are able to navigate the unspoken political tensions in the executive committee meetings."

Clients have often told us, "I thought you were either born with a big non-verbal impact or you weren't. I never knew you could actually learn the specifics that made you seem more engaging."

Well, you can. Authentic charisma is created by exhibiting both confidence and warmth. Visual warmth is displayed in encouraging facial expressions such as smiling, engaged, open body language or laughter.

Showing warmth under pressure has a tremendous impact on your effectiveness

It sounds like a cliché but we often advise clients to smile more at work. So many times we have to ask our clients to lighten up. We ask them if they're storing their smiles for retirement, because they're so serious so much of the time! These clients often decided early in their career to show a stiff upper lip so they'd be taken seriously, but that time is now long gone—they're taken plenty seriously today!

Too often, when we start thinking, our personalities go away. When we start doing tasks, our overt warmth disappears. We are caught up in crossing things off our lists and our connection with others evaporates. A single smile from you can work wonders with others—and with yourself—because your body responds in its respiration, heart rate, perspiration and muscle contraction as though you were relaxed, not tense—just because you're smiling.

Showing warmth under pressure has a tremendous impact on your effectiveness in these times that so often are devoid of hope. Being appropriately warm and pleasant may be a "soft skill," but it gives you tremendous power when you need it most.

You'll lose nothing by expanding your versatility, but you'll gain everything! Some people are so intense; their impact is like drinking orange juice concentrate straight from the can! They need to dilute their impact by flattening their approach to be more effective. Conversely, if you're reserved by nature, share your warmth more broadly by being more expressive.

You may feel awkward with these approaches at first, but don't worry—your brain and body will catch up to these new strategies soon enough.

Seeing yourself as others do really helps you manage your visual reactions; this in turn impacts your vocal reactions. We ask our clients to hang a mirror in their offices so they can see what they look like when they're speaking on the phone. It's much easier to come across more warmly or powerfully when you have someone else to talk to, even if it's just yourself!

Dress, hair and overall appearance are tied closely to executive presence.

Look the Part

Whether you agree with it or not, dress, hair and overall appearance are tied closely to executive presence. Dress and appearance norms differ widely from company to company and from level to level as you rise in authority. Some companies are more formal in their clothing expectations. Others seem to buy all their clothing at the same khaki slacks and polo shirt store. Wherever you work, just upping the ante here slightly makes you seem much more competent. Let go of the idea that people should just accept you no matter what you're wearing or how you appear to the world. It's simply not true.

One client of ours was a brilliant research scientist who routinely bought the socks he wore to work at his local gas station because he was too busy to shop. That's right: they were bright orange hunting socks! Imagine the difficulty his Board of Directors had backing his multi-million-dollar research proposals when he wore those orange socks to his presentation. Whether it's hunting socks, wrinkled shirts, a too-revealing neckline, too much makeup, too little makeup or an inappropriate hairstyle, your authenticity is at stake if you don't look the part. You can have a unique personal style, but you still may need to make adjustments to maximize your effectiveness, based on your organization's culture.

Dress and haircuts are credit card fixes that don't need to get in the way of your perception. If you feel uncertain or lack time, get a personal shopper from a high-service clothing store (for more information, look at SeeingYourselfAsOthersDo.com/reference). You'll feel fantastic in something that fits well, with colors and tailoring that flatter you. It will greatly impact your confidence, your charisma and your sense of presence. We are all just actors on the stages of the companies we're in. Like all actors, we have to wear costumes to fit the parts. Walking on stage in the wrong costume is never a good way to win over an audience!

Posture Counts

Oh, by the way—your mother was right. Posture does count.

Dr. Nili Sachs said, "Posture tells the history of your relationship with your body." Just look around in a mall, a grocery store, or the hallways of your organization. How many people look downright broken, exhausted or defeated as though they had the weight of the world on their backs and it's crushing them?

You can actually look depressed just by your posture. Try it. First, slump in your chair for a few minutes, and then sit upright. Notice how they both make you feel inside. News anchors are taught to sit erectly, but not stiffly, with the small of their backs against the back of the seat. You look at least five pounds lighter and several inches taller when you straighten up with significantly more energy and professionalism.

Actress Jane Fonda was promoting a film she was in on the television talk show circuit just days before her 70th birthday. She walked, sat and stood with the grace of a ballet dancer. Because of her posture, she displayed confidence and looked extremely comfortable in her own skin. It made a powerful non-verbal impact on the audience and the hosts.

Vocal Confidence

The second factor that demonstrates command of the room is your vocal impact. Voices have an enormous impact on people. They can attract or repel. All of us can remember hearing vocal patterns that instantly made us cringe, such as a screechy, whiny or nasal tone. Conversely, we could listen to people such as James Earl Jones or Sean Connery simply read us the telephone book because their powerful, rich, well-modulated voices are so enthralling. Carol was originally a speech pathologist as well as a voice talent herself, so she knows that both these men cultivated their voices—they weren't born with them.

Vocal impact creates up to one third of your initial impression.

Ever given your voice much thought? Most people haven't. They just open their mouths and let whatever falls out come out. They avoid listening to it whenever possible because they don't think they can do anything about it and they don't like how it sounds. Fortunately, you can change the way you sound to others.

Airline pilots are taught to speak with a relaxed, deliberate calmness to keep people calm during a severe storm or when there's engine trouble. Academy Award–winning director Clint Eastwood is known for never raising his voice on the set, which gives him terrific power and presence to calmly command the situation and create a great outcome, even under duress.

Vocal impact creates up to one third of your initial impression. It's significantly more than that if you're on the telephone. Your voice can make a huge difference in your perceived charisma and confidence. In reality, anyone can manage four vocal variables when they speak. They are vocal inflection, rate, volume and emphasis.

The Big Four Voice Changers

Increasing the use of these four vocal qualities will dramatically shift the impact of your voice and how engaging it sounds to others.

1. Inflection is the up and down variation of your pitch, the music of your voice. Your goal is to match your inflection to the meaning of what you're saying for greatest impact. All adults are physically capable of using twenty-four notes of vocal inflection; yet on average, women use sixteen notes while men use only eight.

2. Rate variations involve changing your speed of speech. Speaking too quickly means that you may not be understood or trusted; speaking too slowly means you might be seen as boring or condescending.

3. Volume is about matching your volume level to the environment. Being too loud can seem annoying, overbearing or authoritarian. Being too soft can seem uncertain or weak. You'll be too hard to hear so people check out or talk right over you.

4. Emphasis is having the courage to vary the way individual words are stressed to make your message or vision more compelling. We'll give more detail on emphasis and rate in our "Pause and Punch" technique in Chapter Six on Audience Connection. All great speakers have this approach in their repertoire.

Matching Your Vocal Patterns to the Situation

A Vice President of Marketing for a Fortune 500 company once told us that in his organization, "Vocal inflection is a proxy for passion. If your voice is flat, rushed or lacks interest, you've lost the ability to engage others."

Most people don't grasp how much their voices can encourage, belittle or convey stress to others. We pragmatically coach our clients on how to use their voices for greater impact. One way we help clients understand how their voices sound to others is to have them listen to themselves. We've recorded the voicemail greetings of our seminar participants and played them back. People are shocked at how they sound. They've been known to run out of the room at the break to change their voicemail greetings!

Projecting confidence and charisma vocally to command the room means matching your vocal inflection, pace, volume and emphasis to the situation you're in, the emotion you're trying to convey and the content you're using. The one that initially feels the most awkward at first, yet has the most impact on authentic confidence and charisma, is vocal inflection.

Vocal Patterns that Command the Room

The proper use of vocal variety has tremendous impact on how messages are received. The improper use of vocal tone can damage relationships and result in the opposite outcome from what was intended.

To visualize vocal inflection, think of two oscilloscopes measuring changes in vocal activity. One oscilloscope is active showing a wide variation in vocal delivery with many highs and lows in pitch.

Active Oscilloscope

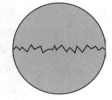

Flat Oscilloscope

The other oscilloscope is flat and calm showing very little variation in vocal delivery.

The active oscilloscope displays how to optimally deliver a positive message. A wider inflection pattern makes a huge difference in how much praise is perceived by the person receiving the praise. Others literally give you more credit for giving acknowledgement if they hear it with more energy in your voice. Try saying the praise message more slowly than your normal pace with more emphasis to stretch-out your words so people can bask in it longer. This delivery approach can help your praise stand out and sink in for people far more. Use of a wider inflection pattern with more sincere enthusiasm will affect your executive presence when you are giving messages of praise or inspiration—you'll immediately seem more inspired and charismatic. We'll give you many other ideas around praise in Chapter Nine of this book, Inspiration, Praise and Motivation.

Conversely, the flat oscilloscope with a calm vocal strength has tremendous power and the ability to capture attention when delivering tough messages. To deliver a difficult message effectively, use a vocal tone with a steady emphasis pattern. Keeping your voice even puts the focus on the message. Most people reverse these two vocal approaches, which mean they are far less effective than they could be when delivering feedback.

When critical messages are delivered with the active oscilloscope, it sounds like, "WHAT were you THINKING? We've GOT to change this NOW!" The receiver walks away resentful, feeling treated like a child and may respond in kind by withdrawing, acting out of fear or perhaps even overtly defying the request. In any case, this commonly used approach in the heat of frustration is counterproductive in the long term. Using vocal patterns that make you sound like an angry parent won't help anyone's productivity.

People often deliver positive messages ineffectively as well. Positive messages using a flat, indifferent oscilloscope create a lose/lose situation. When well-intended people give flat praise, the other person doesn't register the praise. The giver of the praise is not given credit for showing appreciation and the person the praise is intended for doesn't realize they are appreciated.

Leaders need to connect with others, and vocal delivery is one of the most underutilized keys they need to be effective. We have many examples of this single factor making or breaking an executive's ability to communicate authentic executive presence.

In addition to praise and tough messages, vocal inflection communicates many different emotions. Make sure they're the ones you want to share with others. Here are some examples of how voice tone changes communicate emotion.

Flatter Inflection Indicates:	Mid-line Inflection Indicates:	Active Inflection Indicates:
Pain	Empathy	Excitement
Disappointment	Commitment	Passion
Frustration	Caring	Energy
Confusion	Cautious hope	Huge relief
Deep concern	Possibility	Optimism

If you don't like the sound of your voice, you are not alone. There are excellent programs available to help you change inherent vocal patterns. If you would like more information on vocal training programs, go to our website: SeeingYourselfAsOthersDo.com/reference

To be perceived more accurately, here is a summary of how you can have your visual, vocal and content messages be in alignment to create the greatest credibility.

If your content is:	Your face needs to show:	Your voice needs:
Engaged and upbeat	Raised brow, smiling, and nodding	Wider inflection
Interested, trying to understand	Calm, yet engaged expression	Moderate inflection
Frustrated or upset	Neutral expression	Calmer inflection

Now let's talk about how to show presence and charisma with your content, the third aspect of charisma and command of the room to show executive presence.

Clear, Compelling Content

Andy Grove, when he was CEO of Intel, said, "How well we communicate is determined not by how well we say things but by how well we are understood."

The third factor affecting command of the room is content. An author once told us, "Writing isn't about adding words—it's about removing the unnecessary words." This concept is equally true for oral communication, perhaps even more so, because hearing is the weakest learning modality for most adults. That's why fewer, shorter sentences are always easier to understand and remember than longer ones.

In the business world, this concept is frequently violated, but great comics understand it perfectly. Comedian Jerry Seinfeld routinely spends up to five hours taking out one word from a joke because shorter is always funnier.

A former division President we knew from Cargill had a concise response when he was displeased with results from his company heads. He slowly stood up in front of them, took a deep breath and quietly, slowly and calmly said, "I am troubled." Then he walked out of the room. That's it. Do you think that got their attention? There was no question about it. The people in that room were instantly galvanized into action. When asked about it later, the President replied, "They knew why I wasn't happy. I didn't need to beat them up. They knew the numbers as well as I did. I just wanted them to figure out what to do differently than what we had been doing. Sometimes, less is more." As this executive knew, simplicity and clarity have tremendous power to make your command of the room instantly transformational.

Persuasive buy-in isn't achieved by using more words. It's achieved by using fewer words well. Crisp relevance (understood through the OPPOV analysis) is essential to communicate with overloaded people.

The Feeling/Reason/Action Approach

The Feeling/Reason/Action approach allows you to quickly let someone know your feelings about an issue, tell them why you feel that way and ends with a recommendation for action. You can use this approach when you're pleased about something or when you're not at all happy. It's a clear, concise framework to use when you're tempted to use too many words.

The Feeling/Reason/Action approach provides three steps to help you be more compelling and concise.

Step one: State a feeling word to acknowledge how you feel or state a headline of fewer than ten words.

Step two: Briefly tell others why you feel that way based on the facts.

Step three: Tell others what you need, what action you want, or the solution you desire.

You may think that this approach won't work in your organization because feeling words aren't part of its culture, as did Jerry, one of our finance clients who told us, "We're just not allowed to use the 'f-word' in our company—and by that I mean 'feelings!'" On the surface, that may seem to be true, but if you listen to those around you who are the most persuasive, we'd be willing to bet that they are actually slipping in a few of those "feeling words" to make their point with the appropriate passion and intensity.

Not all of the emotions we list here may be appropriate for your company's culture, but a number of them will expand your emotional vocabulary to give your content a compelling impact.

Positive feelings	Neutral/critical feelings
Confident	Concerned
Pleased	Confused
Committed	Curious
Delighted	Disappointed
Excited	Troubled
Satisfied	Apprehensive
Optimistic	Displeased

Here are two examples illustrating how to use this approach to express either critical or positive emotions.

Feeling/Reason/Action example for a critical message.

Use a calm delivery style (flat oscilloscope) and stick to the neutral facts.

FEELING: "I'm very concerned about this strategy."

REASON: "There are too many assumptions that all need to line up to have a chance to be successful and allow us to achieve the goals we agreed to last quarter."

ACTION: "I need us to determine other options to this strategy that have a higher probability of success."

Feeling/Reason/Action example for a supportive message

Use an upbeat delivery style (active oscilloscope) to tell them why you liked what they did so they'll be more prone to give you more of what you want in the future.

FEELING: "I'm very pleased by what you've come up with in this plan."

REASON: "It has all the elements the Board requested, the marketing strategy is in line with our plan, and it is much more innovative than our first attempt. This is the type of creative problem solving I really like to see."

ACTION: "Let's put this into a trial run with the new product."

Less is more. A Ph.D.-level client of ours put it this way during his Change Masters wrap-up meeting with his leader: "I see now that I always wanted to prove to people how much I knew. I now realize I can just give the summary, not all the detail and that's OK. If they want to know more, they can always ask." His leader agreed emphatically, saying, "I don't need to hear all you know. I just wanted to understand if you know enough about this for me to feel you are handling it." Concise communication like this saved them both a great deal of time.

Managing Physical Stress Under Pressure

The fourth factor of commanding the room involves managing physical stress. Our bodies rule how we show up to the world. They will always override our intellect if we're not aware. The two best ways to manage your physical reactions to stress are to breathe and stretch.

Most people breathe ineffectively, particularly when under pressure. Studies tell us that only one in ten people breathe effectively on a regular basis. Many breathe too shallowly, getting at least 30 percent less oxygen than if they were to breathe more deeply. Breathing from your diaphragm helps you relax and get more oxygen to project confident competence.

When nervous, many people use a shallow chest-breathing pattern. This dramatically reduces their oxygen intake, which sends an alarm to the brain. The primal limbic system of the brain senses danger and pumps out adrenaline. The adrenaline makes you more nervous and reduces your oxygen intake even more, creating a vicious circle. Some adrenaline is good, but too much is overwhelming. Typical body reactions from too much adrenaline are:

The two best ways to manage your physical reactions to stress are to breathe and stretch.

Mouth dries up	Lose train of thought
Mind goes blank	Talk too quickly
Perspire profusely	Flat, tense face
Pace back and forth	Tense neck
Vocal inflection too flat	Shaky voice
Too soft in volume	Nervous gestures with hands or feet
Uneasy stomach	Tight gut

You can't counteract the body's primal reaction with your intellect. You need to use a physical approach to calm a physical reaction.

The counter action is to properly breathe with your diaphragm to increase the oxygen intake and cancel the alarm messages sent to your brain. In addition, slower and deeper breathing gives you a richer vocal tone, calmer presence, a relaxed visual expression and allows you to think better. Proper breathing also allows you to stay more alert in meetings and to think more clearly. It makes it much easier to display authentic executive presence.

Stretching is another physical action that helps the body be calmer. Stretching before a meeting or a presentation is an excellent way to prepare the body to perform the way you want it to when the pressure is high. To learn more about stretching techniques and taking care of your body to display executive presence, go to our web site at SeeingYourselfAsOthersDo.com/reference.

Your Command of the Room provides a firm basis for the next attribute of executive presence: how to Leverage Influence and Power.

C OMMAND

L EVERAGE

E XPECTATIONS

A UDIENCE

R ELATIONSHIP

L ISTENING

I NSPIRATION

4

LEVERAGE INFLUENCE AND POWER

When clients walk in the door at Change Masters, they are already delivering strong business results or their companies would not invest in their future. However, getting the numbers is not the only key to success. The most impactful leaders have the emotional competence and ability to influence and persuade without being labeled "political." They know how to use their power in a values-based manner to achieve results that are important to the organization.

One must understand any organization's power and politics to influence and achieve results. It is not an oxymoron to be ethical and political. It is achievable and essential to your success and authentic executive presence.

Unfortunately, too many people misunderstand power and politics, declaring, "I will never be political!" They make judgments about those they see as being political. This rigid attitude limits their own success and ability to learn early lessons about influence and the political skills they need when they move into roles of greater complexity. Every organization is political. Politics may be used for either good or evil. So to ignore the reality of power and politics hurts you and your organization.

Influence and Persuasion

Let's begin with leveraging through influence and persuasion. The purpose of both is to get your audience to reframe their reality by concluding that the action you're urging them to consider is actually in their best interest, not just yours. Here's how we define the differences between influence and persuasion.

Influence is a subtle set of actions, which cause a desired effect in an indirect way. It's a way to lay the groundwork and promote a certain outcome. The dictionary definition of "influence" is to sway or affect a person, thing or course of events, without any direct or apparent effort based on prestige, wealth, ability or position.

Get your audience to reframe their reality.

Persuasion is more overt than influence. It is an active and deliberate engagement with people to get them to embrace a course of action or a point of view. The dictionary definition of "persuasion" is to convince a person to undertake a course of action or embrace a point of view by means of argument, reasoning or entreaty.

We instantly recognize the persuasive eloquence that Ralph Waldo Emerson called "the power to translate a truth into terms perfectly and immediately intelligible to others." This skill requires an understanding of the audience's OPPOV and a well-crafted message that is delivered effectively and appeals to the appropriate emotional motivations.

Your work does not speak for itself. You need to speak up to be heard. No one would expect to build a new product or service, keep it a secret and still have customers buy their offering. People understand the necessity of influencing and persuading customers externally, yet many are poor at doing the same thing inside their own organizations. In fact, when it comes to selling themselves or their team's accomplishments internally, many of our clients resist.

That is why we ask our clients to imagine if the key internal people you need to influence were suddenly clients of their own personal consulting company called "You, Incorporated." We ask them, "Who are the centers of influence that can affect the future of You, Incorporated and its employees the most? How would you interact with your internal customers to develop your book of business? Are you providing your internal clients with things they perceive as having value? Are you waiting for your internal customers to come to you to make things happen or are you reaching out to them?"

Marketing a product just means you relate what you offer to what the customer needs. In the same way, influence, persuasion and internal marketing means you're not assuming others know the value of what you or your team have to offer. You tell them.

Your work does not speak for itself.

One of our clients who initially hated the idea of selling himself or his team's accomplishments was Bob, a rising technology star. When we first met Bob, he was pompous. Within five minutes of meeting him, he had declared, "I don't have to be political. Everyone already knows I work hard and the results are just that good." Bob didn't like it when we told him he was naïve, but he later agreed with us and learned how to be an internal marketer.

Six months after we ended our coaching engagement, Bob told us, "Just the fact that I'm speaking out on important issues makes a difference now in how I'm seen by upper management. In the past, I would have sat back at the officers' meetings and just watched, but now I'm speaking up and acting as a catalyst for our team. Before, selling my ideas and accomplishments was a huge hang-up for me.

"Now, when I'm reaching out to others, I listen first, and analyze what's of interest to the person I'm talking to. I look at their point of view and see how it connects with mine. That's a 180-degree difference from what I used to do! I realize now that they need to know my ideas to help them be more successful. I can feel fine about talking about my team's accomplishments or myself. I thought it would sound boastful or arrogant, but it doesn't. It's just informative. That alone was a huge shift for me. I'm shocked by what I am able to do now. There is virtually no pushback." Bob learned to overcome his misconceptions about the impact of internal marketing and the payoffs in this area led him to be seen very positively by senior management.

Effective Internal Marketer

You can be a more effective internal marketer at any stage in your career. Start by developing a set of clear, compelling statements in sound-bite form. Don't assume others know what your team is doing. This ensures that when you run into someone you want to persuade who says, "So, Tim, what's going on?" you can take advantage of that persuasive moment by describing crisply your key message. Be ready to use these pre-planned marketing moments at the elevator, in a meeting or in the walk down the hall! It's not phony to do so, it's just preparation.

Moreover, don't forget, as you use these crisper, punchier thoughts, you project more positive energy. Senior executives are attracted to positive energy based in fact and results. Lighten up and show your enthusiasm for what you and your group are doing. Inform your face and voice that you're happy! Your energy will be contagious and credible. Once our clients start thinking this way, they come up with all sorts of creative ways to persuade people around them, in big and little ways.

Approaches to Strategic Persuasion

We've talked to many people about how to influence and be seen as strategic leaders in different organizations. Kevin Wilde, Vice President and Chief Learning Officer at General Mills summarized some great techniques for us. He noted, "It doesn't take much time to get more credit for your actions, but you have to dedicate that time every week to make it happen. You can't influence anything if you don't try something."

To promote your ideas, your team or yourself, think about how they uniquely stand out. If you have an innovation that you've grown or are bringing to reality, talk about it more often. Meet with peers and leaders in advance of meetings and tell them, "Here's where we're headed—are we still in synch?" Give them your issue, and ask them their opinion. Explore what they've done that's similar that you might learn. Influence is based on listening and creating dialogue, so ask people, "Tell me about your strategy in this situation—what would you do?" Once they share their thoughts, you can incorporate their ideas into your own so they buy into the approach.

Don't be afraid of letting others play devil's advocate for you. Take the risk to tell people, "Here's my idea, so I need you to challenge me—tell me what you think." Let them know where you're stuck and what you need. Accept that you'll get pushback from people on your ideas, but don't let that stop you from articulating them. Take it in stride, because it means that you'll get buy-in when people get a chance to have their say about your idea. Be passionate with the expression of your idea, but be calm when you're challenged on it. As Kevin noted, influence can't be left to chance.

> **Influence can't be left to chance.**

Influencing Through Chitchat

We talked earlier about the power of understanding OPPOV, or the other person's point of view. It gives you an ability to influence in the art of business social chitchat as well. Several years ago, we shared the OPPOV analysis concept with a client who was technically talented, but also shy. She had risen quickly in her corporation. She was going to fly on the corporate jet with several senior executives to meet with analysts in New York. The prospect of schmoozing for hours with the top brass was paralyzing. Many people would leap at this opportunity, but it was completely out of her comfort zone.

To help her prepare, we did the OPPOV analysis on each executive who would be on the plane. We identified three business talking points for each person. She reviewed *Sports Illustrated, People* and *USA Today* so she could be familiar with the informal talking points likely to be discussed.

The e-mail we got back from our client the day after the analysts meeting said it all: "I wowed them! They all said they had never seen me this engaged and upbeat before! Doing my homework worked!"

When Being Right is not Enough

The need to be right is the undoing of many people who are trying to influence others. Take a lesson from Ben, an operations client of ours. He said, "What I learned through my Change Masters coaching is that sometimes, being right is not enough." Ben had been the champion of a major company initiative to make a significant difference in the product quality across the enterprise. He had done his homework very thoroughly and had every bit of data he could lay his hands on for the analysis. His logic was sound and thorough.

Unfortunately, when he presented his initiative to the head of the corporation, his excruciatingly thorough analysis did not fit with how his CEO liked to receive information. It was rejected because Ben almost immediately lost the interest of the CEO. The opportunity for influence was lost. Ben learned that he could be right and still "get myself into the soup," as he put it. Influence is not only about having a smart idea; it's also about relating it to your audience. It was a lesson Ben will never forget.

Ben learned that to get buy-in, you need to first figure out exactly what it is you're trying to get others to do.

Second, Ben had to realize he was selling.

Third, he learned to pre-sell the benefits and calmly acknowledge any issues by discussing the ideas one-on-one with decision-makers and influencers. By increasing the frequency of relevant communication, he was able to educate and engage his audience about the benefits of his concept. When Ben shared his concepts in advance, he set himself up for challenge, but it was easier to meet those challenges in someone's office than in the boardroom.

Today, Ben is thriving in a new position and delivering persuasive messages more effectively because he was willing to sell his concepts more proactively, be more open-minded and be aware of better ways to be right.

Persuading Teenagers

Ben learned that you couldn't control anyone else's behavior just by the strength of your argument or logic. If you have teenagers, you are experts on this concept! To be successful communicating with the pubertal set you'd better do three things, fast: be relevant, repetitive and creative in your repetition. These are directly connected to persuading or influencing a corporate audience—after all, some of them are just tall teenagers!

1. Be relevant by making the issue relate immediately to what they care about, to their interests or concerns.

2. Be repetitive. Be prepared to say your message multiple times. One senior leader had what she called her "Rule of 22," meaning that some things need to be repeated 22 times before they sink in! After all, how many kids actually wash the dishes the first time they are asked? We had a client recently who reflected what many people feel when he said, "Well, I told them once—they're professionals—I shouldn't have to tell them more often than that." Wrong!

3. Be creative in your repetition. Approach the concept in multiple unique ways to increase the chance of your message registering with them.

Speak the Language of Influence

One way to make influence work better is to anticipate the types of questions your centers of influence will ask. Whether it's your teenager or your boss, figuring out what they're interested in will help you tune into their frequency more quickly. For example, one of our clients, Craig, was continually frustrated by the jarring questions his boss' boss asked him in public settings. They left him feeling unprepared and looking stupid. As we discussed the public-question-asking tactics of his boss' boss, it became clear that Craig only thought through the "what" and "how" questions because that's how he looked at the world. His boss' boss, however, asked "why" questions. Once Craig understood this, he was able to answer the tough questions from above without hesitation and successfully persuade this challenging senior leader.

> **One way to make influence work better is to anticipate the types of questions your centers of influence will ask.**

Build Visibility for Strategic Communications

This concept of speaking the language of influence really rang true for another client of ours, Rick. Rick was not getting any attention for his complex project that required many sign-offs for implementation. He had finally figured out a way to make this project happen in an innovative, streamlined manner with all the appropriate approvals.

Rick was upset that his colleague, Geoffrey, was getting more credit than he was for an idea that Rick considered "fluffy." Geoffrey was getting bigger play for his concept because he was actively involved in marketing his idea. He did things that Rick considered "beneath him," such as inviting senior leaders to collaborate with him in brown bag lunch forums so they could jointly describe the impact to a wider work group.

Rick was blaming the "good old boy" network for this turn of events, but that wasn't the reason at all. We said, "Look, Rick, people are inundated with hundreds of ideas in the workplace, so if you're battling a perception of a well-worn project, you need new, fresh branding of your concept to grab attention." To do so, we helped Rick develop a persuasive communication plan to roll out his "new" concept.

He created a new catchy name to brand his project and clear communications about what the rollout would mean to the business. He made it fun and interesting in a number of ways, including a large sheet cake decorated with the project name that he personally served to employees in the cafeteria. It gave him a great opportunity to tell people about the project and show appreciation to all those who helped make it successful. Rick had the results and built the visibility that made it easier for him to implement the project across the company.

> **You never have to change everything you do all at once.**

One Step at a Time

Sondra, a Director of Operations for a Fortune 500 company, was disturbed when she read her very candid Change Masters survey data and saw herself on screen recreating how she was affecting people as a communicator. She turned to us at one point and said with desperation in her voice, "How do I make all these changes with all these people all at the same time on top of everything else I have to do?"

Well, the reality is that you never have to change everything you do all at once. We asked Sondra to pick three key behaviors to focus on. She was successful with those three and six months later, she was promoted to work with a different department.

Sondra made it her goal to work very well with Bill, who would be significant to her in getting things done. She described the first meeting with Bill: "I sized Bill up quickly to be an expressive person, but one who had a high need to control the conversation.

"The first thing I saw was my resume on Bill's desk. In the past, I would have thought, 'What is THIS supposed to mean?' However, this time I took a deep breath and calmly took the opportunity to ask him if he had any questions about my background. Bill said, 'Actually, I do… how do you pronounce your last name? I'm embarrassed because I don't know how to say it.' That was it. That's the only question he had!

"I told him how to pronounce my name and then made a light-hearted comment about how it looks very different than it sounds. In contrast to my old behavior, I kept it brief and upbeat. I turned the conversation back to some information noted on his white board. I asked him how I might incorporate his information into a presentation I was going to do the following week.

"The thirty-minute meeting turned into an hour! We both learned more than we expected from each other. I knew I had his support. I'm extremely glad I had seen myself as others did so I could be more calm and concise in this and many other situations in my new job."

Breaking the Cycle of Despair

Influence and persuasion are about getting people to change. To change, individuals and companies need to see things differently, but sometimes they get stuck. A Harvard study described this as a "Cycle of Despair."

Harvard found that when people are unhappy because they have a reduced sense of hope, self-worth and safety, they begin a downward spiral. They reach a point where they filter out any positive information that would be evidence contrary to their negative belief. For example, if the newspaper reports that crime is down by 30% and also reports someone was shot during a robbery, the person in the Cycle of Despair will register the person shot as reason to believe life is less safe and not see the reduced crime rate figures. The negative filter promotes the downward spiral.

Organizations behave in a similar way after difficult times. Perhaps market conditions, layoffs or unprofitable years have created a downward spiral. Even when evidence indicates things are getting better, people seem to ignore the positive data longer than is warranted. The direction of the spiral can be reversed, but it takes more than routine communications to do so. You need to reverse the downward trend with messages of hope, self-worth and safety.

In any organization, hope comes in the form of a vision that is clear, compelling and relevant. Worth is seen in praise and recognition both individually and organizationally. Safety is the ability to take prudent risks without retribution if the direction taken is not successful.

Big events can get people's attention and allow them to see the new reality.

Big events can get people's attention and allow them to see the new reality. Once the pattern is reversed, a positive upward spiral can also become self-supporting. It is when organizations have hope, worth and safety that they are most open to constructive change.

It will appear at first that such changes are not taking hold because it literally takes time for people to really see the positive, as Catherine learned.

Catherine was a client who was overwhelmed when she was appointed CEO of an extremely challenged medical services organization. It was trying to reverse its poor reputation for quality in a competitive marketplace. In addition to turning her team around, our client had to influence a very opinionated Board of Directors. At the same time, her team exemplified the "Cycle of Despair." Catherine began by addressing their prior issues in a straightforward, professional way. In so doing, she helped her team believe in themselves again while simultaneously selling their progress to the centers of influence. She sent regular briefings to her Board of Directors on what was going well and how problems were being tackled, then had her staff members present those problem-solving approaches along with her at the Board meetings. This allowed the Board to have hope that solid progress was being made and her team was committed to execution.

Catherine turned the issues around and her team obtained a record increase in the number of contracts due to the quality gains that were made.

In reflecting on it later, Catherine said that her hardest lesson in rebuilding hope was to have the patience and persistence to keep at it. Since she was not a patient person to begin with, she had to learn that hope comes back in small amounts, an inch at a time.

Choosing Your Battles

It is important to be an engaged team player, especially in meetings. There are significant opportunities for most people to improve their perception in this area. Most people fit in one of two meeting participation categories. Either they want to express their extensive opinion on every topic or they are quiet most of the meeting and only speak when they disagree with the direction of a decision. The influence opportunity lies in expressed support for others as often as possible and carefully engaging on contentious decisions.

Decisions fall in two buckets. Choosing your battles recognizes that about 80% of what is discussed is in the bucket that only affects 20% of what is important for you. On the other hand, 20% of the discussions and decisions in meetings are in the bucket where they affect 80% of what is important to you. If you are clear on which bucket the current topic fits in your priorities, you can significantly improve your perception as a team player.

Willingness to Support Others

For the less important 80% of the topics, you can share your view and probably have satisfactory outcomes. When you agree, engage enough to say you are supportive of the decision. However, some will be contentious. When they are, be willing to give in with grace to the other person's view.

You can say something like, "I would rather see us do ABC, but this impacts your area more than mine and I can support your plan to do XYZ."

By choosing your battles, you demonstrate your willingness to support your peers in the meeting four out of five times, even if you disagree. You will be seen as very supportive of you team members.

Willing to Fight the Battle

Now consider something that is part of the 20% high-priority bucket for you. You feel strongly about the outcome and others may disagree. Yours might even be a minority opinion. If you have been graciously supportive of what is important to others in the past, it is more likely that you will get their support when you need it.

You might say, "This is something I feel very strongly about. I believe that if we do not address the issues with C and D, we will all regret it a year from now. I need us to continue to discuss this until we find a way to resolve C and D." We have seen many leaders be much more effective in persuasion using this approach of choosing their battles.

Low-Hanging Fruit—Easy Influence Actions

Influence is an ongoing requirement. A few easy things that have more impact than you might expect are:

Learn their names

One of our clients decided to learn the names of all 202 of the people in his area by putting their pictures on flash cards and memorizing their names along with a few fast facts about them. It allowed him to greet each one personally and share a bit of himself that connected to them as he walked through their areas. It definitely was noticed in a positive way and allowed him to influence people more quickly.

Novel Status Updates

Just taking ten minutes to send Friday e-mails to your team every week, emphasizing what is going well and what's coming up for the next week has been powerful for many of our clients. We call these 5:5:15s—on the fifth day of the workweek, send a message at 5:15 in the afternoon. Your team is starved for information from you. You'll be amazed at the response you'll get from your people just by letting them know what's going on as you will see with our example in Chapter Nine.

Fun Food

If you want to connect with people, food is a great attention-getter. Bringing in pizza or muffins with a two-minute talk about what is working and what the efforts will yield provides a memorable, high return on your nominal investment.

> **Power and politics are neither good nor bad.**

Power and Politics

The second major area of this chapter deals with power and politics, which are closely tied to influence and persuasive success. Power and politics are neither good nor bad, but the way they are used may be judged as good or bad. At Change Masters, we define "power" as the ability to get things done in the organization. "Politics" is the body of interactions and relationships you maintain to get that job done.

It is important to look objectively at politics to maximize your leverage and build authentic executive presence. Political consultant James Carville noted, "You can look at politics as a joke and say, 'What a stupid business. Politicians do absolutely nothing. It's stupid, and I'm not going to play.' Nevertheless, the reality is that this is the game and for all its foibles, these politicians are making major decisions that are impacting wars and schools and roads and people. The political game is the entry point to be able to impact stuff."

To "impact stuff," as Carville says, you have to do the relationship management politics requires. Whether you're working on a church committee, running your kid's soccer team, or leading a national division, "being political" is simply about grasping who needs to know what and when, to get as much done as you can. It's about observing closely to know when something will kick over a hornet's nest and what will calm down hot situations.

Political effectiveness is just one form of power. Your experience, credibility or ability to deliver results are a few additional power bases you might possess. For example, Mahatma Gandhi was the political leader of the Indian independence movement. He was the pioneer of the resistance of tyranny through mass civil disobedience, but his power was in his adherence to total non-violence. Gandhi inspired movements for civil rights and freedom across the world.

Most people would agree that Gandhi was political and that his political achievements were honorable and good. In contrast, we've all seen self-serving "political weasels," but that doesn't mean that avoiding politics is a smart thing to do. Refusal to play the game you're already in is not a mature decision for you or the people you lead. Developing the emotional and task trust to be politically ethical is a tremendous indicator of executive presence.

> **Refusal to play the game you're already in is not a mature decision for you or the people you lead.**

Political Value Systems

The best political players remain grounded in core values while they find a way to be successful in playing the game. They understand the importance of relationships and OPPOV. There is a fundamental and pragmatic choice to accept others as they are and not as we think they should be. There are many factors in making decisions, and logic is only one of them.

Effective leaders may not like parts of the political game. However, they understand that they need to do certain things in order to have the necessary influence in the organization. Things such as choosing which battles to fight; being willing to reach out to someone in the organization that they really don't like; and supporting another department's pet project in exchange for their support of your key project are all part of the game. Within reason, these choices are good for the organization and good for the leader.

One of our clients, Don, said, "Mary is someone who can make the group go with the flow or she can be a roadblock. She likes to be seen as having impact. I include her in things I would prefer not to, because I've learned she is much more cooperative when she feels included." The choice is political to include Mary, but it allows Don to be more effective for the business while still being consistent with his values.

Many people who do not understand the political system react when logic is not the sole factor in a decision by either by refusing to "play the political game" or overdoing it so that it seems smarmy or patronizing. Both approaches are counterproductive to the organization.

The blatantly self-centered political players give politics a bad name and cause the most harm to the organization. The best way to deal with such people is to be better at politics, not by hiding from it.

Power Sources to Get Things Done

We noted earlier that power is your ability to get things done in the organization, but there are many sources of power. Power is relative to a situation. For example, if the issue on the table is union negotiations, the labor expert has more sway. When dealing with your organization's largest customer, the sales expert is likely to be the most powerful person.

Examples of power sources are:
- Knowledge relevant to the subject
- Ability to deliver results
- Persuasive skills
- Ability to communicate purpose and vision

- Acknowledged positional power or authority
- Social background
- Educational background
- Attractiveness
- Referent power
- Money or discretionary budget
- Being a rainmaker
- Personal networks
- Credibility
- Likeability
- The depth of your emotional bank account at work

You may be more powerful than you think.

How Political Do You Need to Be?

The more dependency a leader has on others, the more likely there will be politics involved. The general manager of a small manufacturing plant who has a favorable labor market, multiple options for supplies and a ready market for his products does not depend on others very much to be successful. Therefore, the need for politics is only about 20% of that general manager's job.

Conversely, a CEO of a county hospital system needs to be political 80% of the time. To be successful as the head of the hospital, the CEO needs to negotiate with multiple unions, deal with strong-willed doctors, and manage the relationships with the county, state and federal funders. There is a need to be sensitive to public relations and be seen as a part of the community. The success of that CEO is primarily dependent on relationships.

If the county hospital had to merge with another hospital, politics would probably go up to 95% of the CEO's job. When there is uncertainty, scarcity, unclear processes, ambiguity in direction, conflict or favoritism, the role of politics increases significantly.

Politics is just one form of power to get things done. The situation often dictates how much one needs to be political to be prudent in getting things done. It is very different for the general manager of the manufacturing plant and the hospital CEO.

One symptom of a high level of politics is too many meetings. No matter what the level of political activity in an organization, one common thread that is needed to influence in a political situation is trust.

Decisions Made on Trust

The higher one is in an organization, the more essential trust is in decision-making.

Most important decisions are made based on trust. The higher one is in an organization, the more essential trust is in decision-making. Consciously or unconsciously, a CEO knows she is not getting all the truth about what is really happening with the customer interface. The information is filtered through several levels of reporting for a number of reasons. Even if the CEO goes to the field to ask firsthand, she is likely to get a rosy picture rather than the real truth. So how does the CEO make a decision when she knows she does not have the whole truth and may only have a fraction of the truth?

She has to make decisions based on trust. Trust is based on several things:

- Predictability
- Competence
- Intentions
- Maturity
- "Like me" factor

The "like me" factor reflects the reality that each of us is more likely to trust someone if we think they are like us in some way. If there is a connection, there is more opportunity to influence. We also tend to trust those we think like us, because we expect they will be supportive of our best interests.

We have found that there is both a measure of task trust and emotional trust. Someone who might be predictable in completion of tasks may not be predictable in how they will react emotionally.

Understanding politics and trust makes certain confusing decisions more understandable. We have all seen a situation where two people are competing for the same job. One person is clearly the most competent and yet the other person gets the promotion. The person that was promoted worked for the CEO when they were both in another division. We label it "political" or "good old boy" because the person with the relationship trust won out over the person who is most competent. The reality is there needs to be a certain level of competence, but once that threshold is reached, there are other factors such as predictability and the "like me" factor that are part of the CEO's ability to trust, which tilt the scale to someone the CEO has worked with before. The higher you are on the organization chart, the more trust becomes a critical factor in promotions. It is political. This does not necessarily make it right or wrong.

Make it Easier for Your Boss to Promote You

What if the candidate for promotion is you? You need to have your boss support your promotion. How you are perceived by your potential new boss, your boss' boss and your boss' peers is extremely important. The person promoting you is putting himself or herself at risk by promoting or recommending you.

If everyone on the executive committee thinks you are a great candidate, your boss has a low risk in recommending you. However, if your boss thinks you are a great performer but your boss' peers or boss' boss think you do not have the right executive presence for the new role, your boss is taking a very high risk in promoting you. To increase the likelihood of both receiving the next promotion and then being successful in the new position, you need to build trust and relationships and be appropriately political. If you avoid doing these things because you won't "do politics," you are not ready to be promoted. If you want your boss to support you, you need to support your boss.

Selling Above You

Jill Geisler of the Poynter Institute wisely notes that bosses can become more effective when their subordinates manage them well—and know them well. After all, they do represent a fair amount of influence on your future—why leave things to chance?

> If you want your boss to support you, you need to support your boss.

To this end, Geisler developed a quiz called "Twenty Questions About Your Boss." It tests your depth of knowledge and understanding of the person who has the most direct influence on your success. Could your people answer these questions about you? Can you answer these questions about your boss? Answer as many of these as you can, and consider what it might mean to your effectiveness if you can't fill in some of the blanks.

Twenty Questions about Your Boss

Please identify his or her:

1. Preferred method of giving information to you:
2. Preferred method of getting information from you:
3. Biggest current pressure:
4. Stands for these values, first and foremost:
5. Biggest "hot button":
6. Passion outside of work:
7. Has expertise in:
8. Area lacking expertise in:
9. Vision for our organization:
10. Would be really hurt if someone:
11. Best boss my boss ever worked for:

12. Expects this approach from me when there's a small problem:
13. Expects this approach from me when there's a big problem:
14. Will not compromise when it comes to:
15. Considers a great day at work to be:
16. Handles pressure by:
17. Is respected by her/his bosses for:
18. Respects others for:
19. Has a blind spot about:
20. Thinks I'm great at:

With this pragmatic checklist, Geisler wonderfully captures the essence of a difficult aspect of power and politics. It helps you rethink the concept of influencing up—it's not sucking up, it's just exercising good business and political savvy.

Mature leaders want to know what their people think.

Prioritizing Political Interactions

Johann was a European client from Procter and Gamble who made a tremendous turnaround in his perception through coaching. He reflected on why he had never before done well with corporate politics. Johann told us, "I never prioritized political interactions because they seemed like a total waste of time to me. I never put any value on simple personal interaction to manage relationships. Why should I bother? I'm actually quite shy inside. It was just easier to keep pounding on the people when I had to get the tasks achieved.

"I can see now that it's the moment-by-moment choices that create influence. I was interacting with my team in a way that just wasn't sustainable in the long run. Connecting with people first before you start in on a meeting makes a tremendous difference in productivity, clarity and loyalty.

"Now, when I'm asking questions or challenging others on their thinking, I tell them the headline first. Then I give them a brief context of why I'm asking so they understand the priority it has instead of flooding them with whatever was in my brain at the time.

"As a result of all this, I'm actually sleeping much better and am more relaxed about things since I feel as though I know more of what's really going on. Lightening up just a bit has made a tremendous difference in all parts of my life. I was so serious before, so focused only on results that people never saw the other sides of me. You can't persuade when no one wants to be around you."

Emotional Competence, Influence and Political Savvy

The third aspect of leverage and influence is emotional competence to build trusting relationships through self-awareness, management of feelings, motivation, empathy and social skills.

Emotional competence allows you to know when you just need to stand on your own authority, to show confident, powerful conviction in what you believe—even if that means you need to say no. Mature leaders want to know what their people think, even if they don't agree with it. Being calm, clear, concise and committed to your point of view with emotional competence and maturity can be a tremendously powerful persuasive tool.

Daniel Goleman's research has established that long-term success is based 25 percent on our core intelligence, 25 percent on our technical skills, and 50 percent on emotional competence. This explains why we have all seen intellectually brilliant people fail while those with normal cognitive skills—but stronger emotional competence—survive and thrive.

Emotional competence is an important skill to leverage your internal authenticity and demonstrate your external authenticity. This allows you to make choices that are more effective in demonstrating executive presence, persuasion and making politically savvy decisions. That's what Jim Mitchell found out.

Practical Results Using EQ

When Jim Mitchell was CEO, Chairman and President of IDS Life in the early 1990s, he collaborated with the Executive Vice President of Retail Distribution at the time, Doug Lennick. They were early adapters of emotional competence, putting it to the test under real business pressures, with great business results.

Doug was in charge of the 10,000+ field sales force, Jim in charge of the life insurance group. Jim had determined that 80% of their clients getting financial plans needed to increase their life insurance, but only 25% of these clients were signing up for it. Their research showed that the resistance wasn't about the life insurance product—it was about the emotional discomfort many advisors felt when they had to discuss the realities of death with their clients. They were being emotionally swamped, so they walked away from the business opportunity. Conversely, advisors who were successful at indexing their clients' life insurance to their needs empathetically created trust because of their ability to be aware of and manage their own feelings.

Jim and Doug developed programs to increase financial planners' capacity to understand their own emotions in order to discuss the difficult issues of death with their clients. The quantitative results were enormous. You can hear more about this experience by checking out our in-depth interviews with Doug Lennick on emotional competence at www.SeeingYourselfAsOthersDo.com/reference.

Jim later said in a speech about organizational effectiveness, "Most organizations are a lot less productive than you think. Jay W. Forrester, MIT professor emeritus and one of the leading experts on the dynamics of human systems, suggests that most organizations—both for-profit and not-for-profit—waste some two-thirds of their energy.

"Forrester states that over 90% of an organization's effectiveness is attributable to top management's leadership behaviors, the influence structure of the company, how goals are created and how the past traditions of the organization determine its decision-making and its future.

"But hold on for a moment. Surely, you say, our organization is not wasting two-thirds of its energy. Our employees, under our outstanding leadership, are very productive and engaged. Well… maybe.

"According to a recent survey by Gallup, only 26% of American workers say that they are 'engaged' (loyal and productive). Fifty-five percent are 'not engaged' (just putting in time). Worst of all, 19% are 'actively disengaged' (unhappy and spreading their discontent). These results make Forrester's estimate of two-thirds waste very realistic. I find this very sad. But what a fantastic opportunity!"

> **Emotional competence allows you to filter your intensity so people can move through the stress of a situation—without the stress of dealing with you at your worst!**

You can capitalize on this opportunity with emotional competence, political savvy and influence capability. Gaining more versatility so you can choose different behaviors despite the issues at hand gives you many more options for the future as a persuader with values-based political maturity. Emotional competence allows you to filter your intensity so people can move through the stress of a situation—without the stress of dealing with you at your worst!

Being Authentic and Courageous in the Face of Pressure

Carol will never forget the day she first saw the power of emotional competence coupled with brilliant political timing to influence highly skeptical executives. It was many decades ago, when she was working at The Guthrie Theatre in Minneapolis. The theater was in difficult financial straits and the Board of Directors was trying to decide whether to stage a novel and risky approach to Ibsen's play, *Peer Gynt*. Many were dead set against taking this financial gamble.

The vote was about to take place when Marilyn Carlson Nelson, the persuasive civic and corporate leader who later became the Chairman and CEO of Carlson Companies, made one statement that turned the tide of fear and resistance around completely. Marilyn stood up in front of her frustrated peers, looked them over and paused for what seemed like a very long time. Then she said, "We must do this play, because this play is about the secrets you whisper into your pillow at night."

Carol remembers looking around at the faces of those savvy, brilliant corporate men and women and seeing the shocked recognition of this single truth-filled statement. Marilyn had read their minds and named their common emotional experience with compassionate and profound simplicity. It was courageous enough to sway the group. They voted to do the play.

This choice became an extremely successful undertaking for the theater, with positive repercussions to this day from the innovations they introduced—all because a single courageous woman took the risk to speak from her values and her heart. It was Carol's first lesson in the power of influence by using emotional competence, poise and executive presence under pressure.

C OMMAND

L EVERAGE

E XPECTATIONS

A UDIENCE

R ELATIONSHIP

L ISTENING

I NSPIRATION

5

EXPECTATIONS, STRATEGIC AND TACTICAL

Executive presence is demonstrated by easily moving back and forth between articulating strategic vision and tactical direction. Creating an engaging vision for a goal or project gives the tasks meaning. Tactics make a strategic vision more real and relevant. Mastery of both allows you to create and capture value.

Creating and capturing value is the key role of business. Leaders need to find the opportunity to create value through products, but also through their structure, technology, distribution or quality processes. The way businesses earn revenue is by capturing some of the value created.

Here is a situation that created and captured value. Up until the 1950s and early 1960s, there were thousands of small drive-in restaurants, which varied widely in their quality, efficiency and cleanliness. Around that time, a salesperson named Ray Kroc mortgaged his home and invested his entire life savings to become the exclusive distributor of a five-spindled milk shake maker called the Multimixer. Hearing about the "McDonald's Famous Hamburgers" stand in California, which ran eight of his Multimixers at one time, he wondered why they needed so many. He went to San Bernardino to find out. He was amazed by the assembly line food that was affordable, good-tasting and fast. The restaurant was clean and the service friendly.

Ray Kroc was the first to see the strategic value created in the McDonald brothers' operations and was able to convince them to let him franchise their product, process and cleanliness standards. McDonald's created value by providing consistent national standards to a very fragmented drive-in restaurant industry. Customers and franchisees found value and McDonald's captured value through profits over the years.

> **To create and capture value there needs to be effective strategy and execution of aligned tactics at all levels of the organization.**

Conversely, in the early 1980s, IBM created value, but did not capture value because of tactical error. They were correct in seeing tremendous value provided by bringing standards to the fragmented personal computer business. At that time, there were many personal computer designs and a wide range of quality and function in the industry.

If IBM had waited another eighteen months to establish the standard on their own design, they could have captured a royalty percentage on every PC made. Instead, they rushed to market and set the standard based on Intel and Microsoft, who were very small players at the time. IBM incorrectly assumed they could redefine the standard again in eighteen months when their own proprietary design was released. IBM created the value, but Microsoft and Intel captured the value because of IBM's bad assumptions and tactical error.

To create and capture value there needs to be effective strategy and execution of aligned tactics at all levels of the organization. Divisions and departments need to have strategies and tactics that provide value based on the bigger picture of the organization. In this chapter, we will talk about how to be more effective in the communication of expectation, strategies and tactics at all levels.

Execution Tactics—Communicating Clear Expectations and Tough Messages

To capture value, you need to communicate clear expectations and deliver tough messages. Tough messages are any messages that you don't like to give or the other person doesn't like to receive. Many people think of tough messages as the extreme of a termination discussion, but any corrective feedback falls into the category of a tough message.

There's a wide range of expectations that need to be set, from fairly simple and straightforward to multi-year-long projects that need to be worked through in multiple, complex discussions.

Here's how we instruct clients to deliver them, using our Expectation Pyramid Model.

Expectation Pyramid

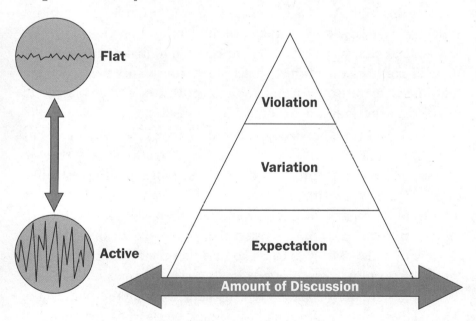

The Expectation Pyramid starts at the base with Tier One, called "Expectation Setting." Tier Two is called "Variation" and at the top is Tier Three, called "Violation."

The width of the Expectation Pyramid represents the amount of discussion you need to have at each of the three tiers. The pyramid height represents the vocal delivery style of the message. It begins with an active, energized conversational vocal style at the bottom. If you need to escalate the message, your voice needs to move to a flatter, calm but firm delivery pattern with a shorter message.

Tier One—Expectations

In the first tier, setting expectations, you're establishing a contract with the other person. The intent is to make sure there is a clear agreement on what will be accomplished, when it will be completed and what guidelines will be used (such as communications, budget or resources). The conclusion should be a freely-agreed-to set of expectations with commitments to action.

To achieve clear expectations there needs to be give and take in the conversation. You need to listen for understanding. Questions such as "With the other things you are working on right now, are you able to commit to this date?" are crucial to make sure you have a solid contract established that both parties can agree to. There may need to be some negotiation of priorities and resources to make the expectations and commitments realistic.

The base of the Expectation Pyramid shows the longest discussion in the first tier, with the most active interaction of any stage in the model. For large projects, the first meeting might be establishment of the goals with a discussion about what success will look like from multiple viewpoints. You might then request that the other person or team lay out a written plan to achieve the objective and review that plan with you to make sure that their translation of the goal into action steps properly reflects your expectations. Clear milestones should be set as well. If there are multiple phases, the shared expectations for each phase should be clearly articulated.

The time invested in creating clear expectations up-front has a high return on investment. Those who have implemented this approach have reported it has saved them significant amounts of time because they are not going over the same issues repeatedly and they are getting more of what they expected.

Expectation Pyramid Example—Tier One

Let's work a simple example of a one-week project to show how this approach works. Bob is the manager and Jim is a subordinate. It is Monday.

Bob: Jim, I just found out that Mary wants our group to create a presentation for her regarding the ABC project that she will be giving to the executive team meeting next Monday. I want you to get some exposure with that group, so I want you to take the lead on this. We'll be using the same format that Mary used last quarter. I will get you the new financial information she needs to incorporate. You will need to check with Bill and Pat on the latest information on ABC from their departments.

I know it's very busy right now and you plan to leave early on Friday for your summer place, but I need you to have the completed presentation to me by Friday at noon so I can go over it before I meet with Mary on Monday morning to review the presentation with her.

This is a high priority. Will you be able to get the presentation to me no later than noon Friday with all the other things you are working on?

Jim: Projects X and Y are also due this week. If I can move one to those to next week, I will be able to get the presentation done by Friday morning.

Bob: If we move delivery of project Y to Tuesday, will that give you enough time?

Jim: That should work.

Bob: I want to position you as the key communicator on the ABC initiative over the coming year. This is the first step in that direction. I think it will position you well when it comes to your promotion.

If you need my help to get Bill or Pat to give you the information for their departments, let me know by Wednesday. I will have my information for you tomorrow. Just stop by and I will go over the charts with you. We can talk about the rest of the presentation when we have our one-on-one meeting on Wednesday.

Jim: That will work.

Bob: OK, just so I know I was being clear, Jim, can you summarize what you understand we've agreed to so we are sure we have the same expectations?

Jim: I will have the completed presentation for Mary to you by Friday at noon. I will get last quarter's presentation from Mary's assistant and the update information from Bill, Pat and you by Wednesday. I will move the due date for project Y to next Tuesday.

Bob: Great, that is correct. I think this will be good exposure for you with Mary.

Often this is all you need to do. With this level of clarity the requested action is done. You've communicated, you have a contract and you should get results. However, if you don't get what you want, you escalate to Tier Two, the variation to the contract.

Tier Two—Variation

The variation level of the Expectation Pyramid is when you have reason to believe that things are not on track to meet the objective, yet the goal is still achievable. You want to obtain recommitment to the goal and introduce or remind them about the consequences if the agreement is not kept.

On the Expectation Pyramid, the variation tier has a shorter base, meaning there's less conversation. From a delivery perspective, it is halfway up the expression scale, meaning that the vocal tone is flatter and firmer than tier one, but not a monotone.

Before the deadline, with enough time to recover, determine why there was a variation from the agreed-to expectations. Stay neutral in your visual, vocal and content approach, state your reaction, and restate the mutual commitment.

Briefly describe the gap between your expectations and your observation. Verify the gap exists, ask for any reasons for the variation and after you hear them out, state the consequence of not meeting expectations. The other person then needs to recommit to the contract.

Tier Two Example

Bob: Jim, I am concerned that you did not come by for the updated financial information on ABC yesterday. Are you on track with Mary's presentation?

Jim: I know, I was planning to work on it yesterday, but I had a flare-up with project X that took most of my day. Bill and Pat have not responded to my request for information. It's not a problem. I have all day Thursday blocked off to work on the presentation.

Bob: Jim, this presentation is a higher priority than project X. I want Mary to see you as the lead communicator on the ABC initiative. You can't afford to miss on this one. Send me a copy of what you have completed by the end of the day on Thursday. It is essential to have this presentation done by Friday at noon. If it is not done by noon on Friday, I need you complete it Friday afternoon and work this weekend to get it done if necessary.

Jim: I will get it done. I have time set aside tomorrow.

Bob: Do you need me to contact Bill and Pat for you?

Jim: No, I am on it.

Bob: Here are the updated financials. Be sure that you follow the format Mary used last quarter, and remember, if it's not done by Friday, you'll be working this weekend.

In this example, Bob identified his reason for concern. He introduced the consequences of needing to cancel plans to leave early on Friday and work on Saturday if the presentation is not done by Friday. He knows Jim wants more visibility but also knows that he loves going to his summer place. Bob obtained the renewed commitment to have the presentation completed by Friday noon. Jim has recommitted to the objective and understands the consequences. Bob's vocal delivery tone of the message expresses concern and his content is more crisp and commanding.

Tier Three—Violation

The third tier—violation—is a firm stand that we call "drawing a line in the sand." This is the top of the pyramid, where the amount of discussion is short and the delivery of the message is flat and unyielding. The delivery can seem a little harsh at first, but delivering a concise and firm message allows the focus to be on the expectation that has been agreed to and the consequences of not meeting the expectation.

Once the person in question acknowledges the expectation and the consequence, the conversation is over. Don't listen to excuses for not performing. This is a time we advocate interrupting excuses by asking them if they understand the stated expectation and consequence. When they say, "yes," the conversation is over. Any more discussion becomes counterproductive. You rarely have to go to this stage, but it's very useful to have in your repertoire. Let's look at how tier three plays out.

Expectation Pyramid Example—Tier Three

It is now late Friday morning. Bob has not yet received a copy of the presentation that Jim promised to send on Thursday evening. Bob goes to Jim's office.

Bob: Where are you on the presentation for Mary?

Jim: I had another crisis yesterday on project X, but I am working on the presentation right now. I'll be done really soon.

Bob: Jim, you agreed to have the presentation done by noon today. I need you to stay this afternoon to finish it and come in tomorrow if needed.

Jim: I have family plans to go to our summer place this afternoon.

Bob: Then you need to complete the presentation in a quality fashion by noon. Do you understand?

Jim: But I...

Bob (interrupting): Do you understand?

Jim: Yes, I understand.

Bob: Good.

And with that, the discussion is over. Bob immediately leaves Jim's office.

This is deliberately a short discussion because you don't want any prolonged dialogue about reasons or excuses. When expectations and consequences are clear, more gets done with less hassle. People are also less likely to test your resolve in the future.

A Vice President of research at Corning International told us that the use of this Expectation Pyramid saved him 20% of his time every week because he was not going over the same issues repeatedly. This approach can be done at any level, both at work or at home. Setting clear expectations is how you start, but you also need relevant consequences to make this approach work effectively.

Consequences—The Time Saver

Appropriate consequences are an integral part of the escalation process in delivering tough messages. Understanding the Other Person's Point Of View (see OPPOV in Chapter Two) is helpful in determining the consequences, because negative consequences are about giving someone more of something someone does not want or less of something they do want.

To retain credibility, consequences must be something that:

1. you have control over
2. is relevant to the other person, and
3. you are willing to execute upon if the objective is not achieved.

The example of Bob and Jim we just reviewed was for a boss and subordinate. Bob was able to require that Jim work on Saturday if he was not done with his commitment on Friday because it was within his control to do so. There are other ways to effectively use consequences, such as the approach used by Tom Mungavan.

Consequence Escalation Example

Tom was brought in as a leader to turn around a computer systems development group with Target Corporation. He had to implement a major systems development project with challenging timelines to meet critical business needs. The projects had to be completed on time. Meanwhile, George, the project leader, liked autonomy.

The consequence that Tom used successfully with George was to increase his direct supervision with George when the project was behind schedule. First, there were weekly meetings, but the results were still not satisfactory, so Tom upped the ante to meet with George three times per week. It escalated to the point that there were daily meetings at 7:30 A.M. to review progress. George hated it and Tom wasn't thrilled either, but it caused George to find a way to get back on track. As the schedule situation improved, the meetings were reduced a step at a time to once per week. That was an effective consequence for George as well as a way to timely resolve issues.

Tom had another leader, Jennifer, who liked all the attention she could get for her projects. The daily meetings would have been a reward for her. The consequence that worked well for George would not have been appropriate for Jennifer. Being thoughtful about the individual's motivation is important in selecting consequences. Looking at their OPPOV makes it easier to select consequences.

Consequences Without Authority

It is easier to see the consequences for subordinates or children than it is for spouses, peers or bosses, where you don't have direct authority, but the model still works.

Suppose you are working with a team of peers and everyone has agreed to certain actions to complete a project. One of your peers agreed to provide you with a key deliverable by Friday. Your consequence could be, "You know, we all agreed in the meeting that this was going to be done by the end of next month. If I don't have your piece of it by the end of this week, I will need to escalate this issue so that everyone who was in that meeting knows that we are not going to make our date." Your consequence is to escalate the issue to the group. You might have another situation where you have a mutual boss that you will escalate to if commitments are not kept.

You can give your boss consequences as well. You might say, "When I agreed to the year-end delivery date, it was with the understanding that I would have the resources by the end of this month. If the resources are delayed, I will have to withdraw my commitment to the year-end deadline. Every month we delay, the end date will move by one month."

You build your authentic executive presence by setting clear expectations and holding people accountable.

Upside-down Pyramid

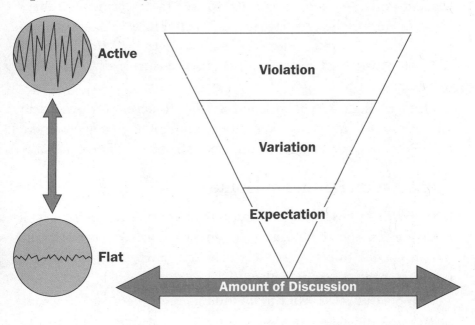

Many people actually flip the Expectation Pyramid upside-down. They spend a short amount of time on the expectation with a flat, indifferent vocal pattern. When things aren't going well they escalate rapidly to the violation level, using an angry vocal tone, talk longer than they should and even bring up things that are not helpful to the situation.

The other person will often react with "You never told me that," or "That is not what I thought you wanted," or "I thought that Project B was a higher priority so I delayed this objective."

The worst part of the upside-down pyramid approach is that the other person walks away focused on your behavior of blowing up, being unclear or too demanding, rather than on the fact that they did not do what was expected. They are the victim and you are the villain.

An executive with a long history of contentious interactions with her team reported implementing the Expectation Pyramid and said a year later, "Today, no one would say I attacked them without notice. No one has been surprised by any critical feedback I had for him or her. In retrospect, I should have taken more people on earlier in my senior leadership role than I did. I learned when I maintained relationships with no surprises I could be tougher on results."

It takes maturity, patience and wisdom to develop strong clarity and persistence in setting expectations and holding people accountable. But it will be worth it to gain your authentic executive presence.

Expectation Setting at Home

Barb decided to use the Expectation Pyramid on her most challenging issue: her son's bedroom! Her son, Jason, was 13 years old and Barb argued with him every week about cleaning his room. In the past, it was the classic dialogue:

Barb: Jason, clean your room today.

Jason: I did clean my room.

Barb: You call that clean? Go clean it again!

After learning the Expectation Pyramid, Barb sat down at the kitchen table with Jason on a Saturday morning. She reviewed the expectations and the consequences. They worked together that morning on cleaning Jason's room. When they were done she said, "*This* is what I mean when I say the room is clean." That was the clear description and a shared expectation, which included:

1. The bed was made with clean sheets.
2. All the dirty clothes were in the laundry room.
3. Things were put away and off the floor.
4. The floor was vacuumed.
5. The wastebasket was emptied.
6. All the soda cans were in the recycling bin.

The consequences were that if Jason did not have his room clean by noon on Saturday, he could not go out with his friends on Saturday night and he could not have friends over to his house. The consequence was clear and one that Jason *definitely* cared about.

You train people how to treat you. Make sure they are treating you the way you desire.

In the subsequent five years until Jason left for college, Barb did not have a single argument about cleaning his bedroom. She invested a little time up front in setting clear expectations and reaped the benefits of saving time, reduced stress and a much-improved relationship with Jason.

One final note on consequences, think about how you might be training people to avoid doing what you ask. If you say, "I can't trust people to get it done right so I do it myself," you train others to take advantage of you. If they don't do it the way you want it done, they are rewarded because you do it for them. You train people how to treat you. Make sure they are treating you the way you desire.

Using Anger to Clarify Expectations

We get angry when we have an expectation and it is different from what we observe. If the gap is large and it is something we care deeply about, we are very angry. Anger can help us clarify expectations. Think of "anger" as a range of feelings from frustration to rage. It represents any situation where you are not happy with what's going on around you, for whatever reason. To deal with anger and to clarify your own expectations use the four expectation questions:

1. What exactly did I expect?
2. Is my expectation reasonable?
3. Have I clearly communicated my expectation?
4. Has the other person agreed to the expectation?

Once you have completed these four questions and you have agreement on the expectation, you have a "contract" that forms the expectation base of the Expectation Pyramid. You are now in a position to escalate if your expectations are not met.

Your personal preferences or the way you did it at another company may not make it a reasonable expectation.

Going through these questions will often reveal that your expectation was not expressed or was not agreed to by the other person. Using these questions allows you to move calmly toward shared expectations, which demonstrates maturity and executive presence.

Reasonable Expectations

One area of confusion is often how to define a reasonable expectation. When you ask the question "Is my expectation reasonable?" be ready to be very objective. Your personal preferences or the way you did it at another company may not make it a reasonable expectation. We all have personal preferences and they differ. Be sure your expectations are based on the business need.

For example, when we started Change Masters, we had a reception area that was 20' by 20'. There was a desk for our receptionist. She would work on client files and they would occasionally stack up on her desk. Tom looked at those files every time he walked in the office and said to himself, "You know, that doesn't look good and I don't like how it impacts client confidentiality. I'm going to do something about it."

So he had a cherry wood desk made, one that he called the "tank," where the receptionist's head and shoulders are all you can see above it, because it covers everything up. When the "tank" was all set up, it looked fantastic. Tom was delighted—problem solved! He'd never have to deal with it again.

But what do you suppose happened when Tom walked in the next day? You guessed it; there were piles of files stacked up on top of the "tank" that were even more visible than ever. They were now almost at eye level! Tom was not happy. He started through the four expectation questions:

1. What exactly did I expect?
    His expectation was that no files would be visible—his observation was that files were more visible than ever.

2. Is my expectation reasonable?
    Absolutely.

3. Have I clearly communicated my expectation?
    Absolutely not. Oops.
    Tom had a picture in his mind and it was so obvious to him. After all, why would he buy this new desk if he wanted files to show? When he approached our receptionist and said, "You know, Mary, when I bought this desk, one of my goals was to not have these files visible when someone walks in the door," Mary's immediate reaction was, "Oh, that makes sense."

4. Has the other person agreed to the expectation?
    Just like that, she agreed to the "contract."

Now if Tom had come in the next day and there had been files stacked up, then he would be escalating with a tough message and a contingency. However, the files were not there the next day. In fact, they were never visible again.

Going through the four questions of expectation setting allows you to focus first on the expectations, and not on the anger. Otherwise, it would be easy for Tom to walk in and get very upset with Mary for the files being visible. What we expect is not always that obvious to others no matter how reasonable we judge our expectations to be.

Strategic Communication

> Focus first on the expectations, and not on the anger.

Now that we've reviewed facets of tactical communication, the second part of this chapter revolves around strategic communication. Being able to move fluidly between strategic vision and tactical execution is an important mark of executive presence. Your tactics need to be in the context of your strategy to be clearly understood by the organization. Your strategy needs to have effective tactics to enable your vision to become a reality. For many of our clients, success in this area is based on how well they speak the language of strategy. They need to help people understand their strategic thought leadership.

Can You Teach Strategic Thinking?

When we are grooming leaders, it is common to have a client who is very good at getting results, but there is a lingering question about his or her ability to be strategic. Of course, there are people who are just not good at thinking strategically. If that's the case, there isn't much we can do to change that ability.

However, about 80% of the time when we deal with someone where strategic thinking is in question, we find people are much stronger strategic thinkers than they appear to be. Often the core issue is that the strategy is so obvious they don't think they need to articulate the strategy. Some have even said, "I thought it would be insulting to their intelligence to state the obvious." If that is the situation, we can help them tremendously.

Carla learned this lesson well. When we met her, she was an outspoken technology executive. She was widely respected for her expertise, but she was seen as far too intense and detail-oriented. In fact, her colleagues described her as a "tactical bulldozer." She hadn't grasped the concept that as you rise in a complex organization, things can take longer to accomplish since the ramifications of a mistake are far greater. More perspective and time is often required to make sure the ship doesn't hit an iceberg.

This idea didn't jive well with her intense personality that was focused on tactical productivity. That's when Carla's sponsor said to her, "If you're going to go down the stress road, make sure there's something significant at the end of the road. If you can't do the basic tactical execution steps, like collect money or ship product, get worried—for everything else, get some strategic perspective before you react."

Carla's strategy was so obvious to her, but she loved crossing things off her tactical list. She needed to communicate her strategy in a way that clearly tied it to the tactics she was implementing. She also learned how to calm her delivery of her strategic communication messages. The impact was dramatic in terms of how her strategic competence was viewed. The day she was promoted to Vice President, she sent us the announcement, "You can put this in your scrapbook of successes. I finally made it."

Expanding Strategic Thinking in Others

Randy Darcy, Executive Vice President and Chief Technical Officer at General Mills, said that he asks certain questions to increase versatility in strategic thought leadership. He wants people to think broadly and deeply rather than being focused on just a single solution. His goal is to make sure they've thought of the ramifications of both the tactical and the strategic implications in their immediate areas of responsibility and cross-functionally. As he put it, "Nothing at General Mills speaks louder than results. I'm trying to get people to comprehend the real risk profile around their decisions, because most of the time issues aren't around being risk-averse, it's that we didn't define the risk appropriately in the first place. Often within a large, complex organization, part of making a major change is in getting small wins, demonstrable risk that can be reapplied to build your case. That's how you change the corporate world—clever, smart execution. Around here, it's 50% about the quality of your idea and 50% how you get it done.

"Most of the time, you aren't making a decision that will just impact you. It will also impact many others. So, I'll ask them, 'Did you talk to Carol about it? She'd have a perspective that's very valuable on this topic.' If the answer is no, I have them do so. If the answer is yes, we talk about it. It allows me to coach them on cross-functional boundaries and collaboration."

Complexity with no immediate relevance turns people off.

To coach people on this, Randy says to them, "OK, I see what you've got on this piece of paper, and you've got a list of 115 reasons, but sit back for a minute and be the CEO. Tell me why you would want to do this. Why do you think this is so important?" He has them describe their concept in example form—when they do so, they get clearer and so does he.

To communicate an idea or action effectively to people, it's all about clarity and simplicity, always bearing in mind who you have to persuade and why. Complexity with no immediate relevance turns people off.

Speak the Language of Strategy

Any great employee is on the lookout for what adds value to the boss and the company. Just listen to those who have impact in meetings—see what they're saying and how they get others to react. Re-evaluate what you say to senior leaders or your teams in this way.

One of our clients, who had resisted using what she called "Corporate BS-speak," later recalibrated her thinking when she saw herself on camera. She said, "I've learned that if speaking the language of strategy contributes value and demonstrates that I understand strategic thinking on a more subtle level, it's worth it since it ultimately benefits the organization, my group and me." We've found that you'll sound strategic by asking one great question at the right time in a thoughtful, calm manner.

Here are some questions that allow you to glean more strategic information:

- How does this fit with our stated mission?
- What are we missing in this discussion?
- What is the unspeakable truth?
- What's going on from a broader perspective?
- How would a startup entrepreneur with money go after our market?
- How might our competitors react if we do this?
- What are the underlying assumptions we are making?
- How sure are we that the customer will accept this approach?
- Where are we right now in this situation compared to where we intended to be?
- What happens if we continue doing it the way we are now?
- What questions should we be asking right now?
- If we were sure we would be successful, what approach would we take?
- How much longer will we continue on this path before we change?
- What can we learn from what other organizations have already tried?

Using broad-based questions can show others you are thinking strategically.

Case Study: Do Less to Achieve More

A finance executive from Wells Fargo, Jerry, learned a lot about his need to develop a stronger strategic orientation in a new role. Jerry had started out as a lender, an individual producer who had hustled hard for his book of business. Now, sixteen years later, as his business line was projected to double again, he chose coaching to help him deal with this success.

Jerry received feedback saying he was too tactical, mired in detail. He was losing the opportunity to be crisp, decisive and show executive presence. Jerry saw how he looked on video as he rambled on, taking almost seven minutes to answer one question we asked him! We had him compare how he looked when he asked a single strategic question in a slower, quieter manner. He was stunned by how much more confidently and powerfully he appeared with a simpler approach.

After seeing himself as others did, Jerry said, "There's a huge difference between your perception and your intent. It's hard to understand what others' perception is when all along your intentions feel good inside. This clears up the confusion I had around how they had interpreted me so differently than I intended!"

There was another level of confusion as well. On camera, Jerry looked more matter-of-fact, self-assured, confident, older and more mature than he perceived himself to be. Inside there was a different guy. In Jerry's mind, he was still the blonde, freckle-faced kid who was the youngest of six, always trying to earn his stripes. It had made him push and try to prove himself his whole life. Because of this, when Jerry was intense, his use of passion was totally misperceived as being really ticked off.

We asked Jerry to break a lot of old, baked-in patterns that were no longer useful to him. To help him with this transition, we had him identify two people he respected who represented executive presence in his mind. He came up with two people—a CEO client of his named Mitchell and a man named Lawrence, a senior executive in his company who had responsibility for national lending practices. They both had a commanding presence. They were both under tremendous pressure, but neither came off as rattled at any time.

Jerry said, "I was always uncomfortable with silence when I was under pressure, so I'd start to prattle on tactically, but Lawrence and Mitchell own the room because they're clear and self-assured. They both just look at you expectantly until you answer the question. They never ramble. They're much more comfortable with silence than I am. I realize now how they just ask the strategic question or make the strategic statement and expect others to fill in the tactical blanks."

We asked Jerry to keep this "Lawrence and Mitchell" filter in his head in moments of tactical temptation. He needed to breathe and act as if he was operating in their shoes. Doing so allowed him to talk less and listen more; he wouldn't divulge so much so readily; he'd speak strategically instead of just tactically and he wouldn't ramble and confuse people.

When Jerry first started to explore a more strategic approach, he noted, "It's hard to find a middle ground when you've been raised in a black-and-white world. I've always thought I was expected to know everything from A to Z. The Decade Shift profile really helped me see that it's unrealistic to keep believing that. Ironically, I've preached this to people for years, but I had never mastered it myself."

Jerry's final words were reminiscent of Bill George's when he said, "I now see so clearly that making these strategic changes will evoke change in those who work for me. I've tried to cover up my weaknesses from people. I wasn't fooling them; I was just fooling myself. I know now that was a mistake." It was a testimony to balancing tactical and strategic skills to create a strong, steady sense of executive presence. Jerry learned a lesson many of our clients have learned over the years, that communication, even difficult communication, is the lifeblood of leadership.

C OMMAND

L EVERAGE

E XPECTATIONS

A UDIENCE

R ELATIONSHIP

L ISTENING

I NSPIRATION

6

AUDIENCE
CONNECTIONS

Outstanding presentation skills can dramatically influence the direction and commitment of an organization. Even small group presentations in front of the right audience may be pivotal. There is tremendous power in a presentation that connects with the audience, persuades and demonstrates executive presence.

There is a deep need for clarity and crispness in presentations by executives who are already under extreme time pressure. Leaders with authentic executive presence present ideas quickly, compellingly and simply.

Most people miss significant opportunities to lead because they make their presentations too complicated and do not properly prepare. To build your audience connection, you need to understand the audience, prepare your focused message and commit to a powerful delivery.

Understand the Audience

To make your presentation relevant, you must take time to think through the needs and concerns of your audience. Use the OPPOV analysis from Chapter Two as a preliminary step. It helps you understand what the audience needs from your presentation, what concerns them and how you need to structure the content of your message to be most effective with them, using a memorable open and close.

Someone who knows this very well is Harvey Mackay. He is the master of looking at the other person's point of view in presentations. Mackay is a best-selling motivational writer, as well as an acclaimed speaker and businessperson. One of Harvey's keys to persuasion success is learning everything he can about his audience in advance.

Harvey is also a world-class salesperson who founded a small envelope company, Mackay Envelope, at the age of 26 that grew to become one of the leading direct-marketing companies in North America. His influence and persuasion skills helped bring the Super Bowl to Minneapolis—in January!

Harvey knows his audience so well, he can adjust to their needs quickly, and he always fully commits himself emotionally to the moment. His message is delivered with unflappable aplomb and a twinkle in his eye.

Carol's father, Stefan Ingvarsson, worked for Harvey as his CFO many years ago. At one point, Mackay Envelope badly needed a loan for expansion of their plant. Stefan was trying to tell Harvey all the reasons why the bank might say no. After going into detail, Stefan felt he was getting nowhere with Harvey, so he packed up his papers, saying, "Harvey, I know you don't like what I'm saying."

Harvey leaned forward, a wide smile on his face and said, "Keep talking, Stefan, keep talking—I'm listening!" What Harvey was actually doing was using Stefan to help him do his homework for his presentation so he could overcome the resistance of the bankers. He welcomed Stefan's challenges because they allowed him to figure out how to counter the bankers' concerns when he presented to them. As a result, he successfully obtained the loan.

Thinking about your audience helps you adjust the detail level accordingly. Here are some questions to consider:

- What is the awareness level of your audience about your issue?

- Are you there to inform or educate?
- Do they understand the issue?
- Are they believers or detractors?
- Are they able or ready to take action?
- Why should they want to listen to what you're talking about?
- What's in it for them? What benefit will they gain?
- What problem will it solve for them?

Ask other people their opinions on these as well, so you're not making assumptions based on your perspectives. Once you've answered these questions, then you're ready to start to put your remarks together.

> **The best return on your time for a presentation is your preparation.**

Message Preparation

The best return on your time for a presentation is your preparation. Professional speakers spend one hour of preparation and rehearsal for every minute of finished content. You can't take that kind of time to prepare, but you must rehearse aloud.

It's one thing to think an idea through in your head or on a slide, but it can be an entirely different result when it comes out of your mouth. Don't kid yourself into thinking you can "wing it." Skimming through your PowerPoint slides does not constitute a rehearsal. We have seen far too many examples of how that approach has been career-limiting, meaning that a major exposure opportunity ended up underwhelming the audience. You are giving a performance when you present. Even the best Broadway actors would fail on opening night if they did not rehearse.

Any rehearsal, done aloud, preferably in front of a mirror, will give you the added advantage of focus and confidence. As the actor Michael Caine said, "Rehearsal is the work so the performance can be the relaxation." If you can video record it and watch it, you're much better off rather than tinkering with a special effect on your

PowerPoint slides. This investment of time on your delivery will reveal areas of fine-tuning in your content and provide you with the best possible return on your time that you could make.

The most common content issues in presentation are:

1. There is no message
2. There are too many messages, or
3. The message comes last.

These are all symptoms of not spending the time needed to prepare.

Clear and Concise

A simple and clear presentation is always harder to prepare than rambling and unfocused one. Mark Twain is attributed with saying, "If you want me to speak for three days, I need an hour to prepare. If you want me to speak for an hour, I need three days to prepare." Investing the time to create a simple and clear presentation will be very rewarding in terms of results.

> **What's the one thing you want this audience to know or to do when they leave?**

The key question we ask of anyone coming to us for help in putting together their presentation is, "What's the one thing you want this audience to know or to do when they leave?" It can be a tremendously difficult question for our clients to answer, since they have so many ideas of what they want people to do as a result of hearing them. This key question is the most important question.

Most people make the content of their presentations too complicated. Content is best when it is relevant to the audience, creatively redundant and easy to follow. It is typically going to be shorter than you think it needs to be. Try cutting your presentation by 50% and see what is essential to retain. If it gets the point across clearly, you're done! You don't have to prove how much you know about a topic in a presentation.

We ask our clients to pick three short, declarative sentences that describe their presentation concept, for instance:

1. We believe the project will meet its deadline.
2. The project will generate a 15% increase in sales next year.
3. We need to keep this project as our main focus in order to achieve this result.

Make three points the backbone of your presentation by getting them out three times during your talk. Having such a clear focus helps you stay on track and helps your audience understand what you're saying.

Think of the great presentations from the past. They are memorable because they were simple, significant and instantly meaningful. How simple? Look at these examples:

- Abraham Lincoln's Gettysburg address was a mere 269 words and less than 3 minutes long.
- Winston Churchill's "Blood, Sweat and Tears" speech was only 627 words.
- Dr. Martin Luther King, Jr.'s "I Have a Dream" speech was only 1,667 words.

Keeping it simple also makes you more flexible. In fact, professional speakers always have at least three speech lengths. They know that at anytime they may be asked to cut their presentations and they know just where to cut from a half day to an hour—even to five minutes, if necessary!

We know of one such speaker who was asked to do just that. The overall program for the conference was running long. The hot catered lunch had just arrived, 45 minutes early. The meeting planner desperately asked him to cut his 60-minute presentation down to five minutes! He didn't get flustered.

Instead, he graciously agreed, then calmly went in front of his audience and said, "Ladies and gentlemen, I've just been informed that your delicious lunch has arrived a bit early and we want you to enjoy it while it's warm. I've been asked to cut my remarks to five minutes, so in conclusion..." The audience broke out in laughter and applause. He literally just gave them his final remarks. He later told us, "I think it was one of the most effective presentations I've ever delivered!"

For important presentations, be prepared for a five-minute version. We have seen major presentations to the Board of Directors be cut from 30 minutes to five minutes with little notice. If you have a clear, compelling message, shorter content may make your presentation even better.

The human brain is more capable of remembering three points than five or ten points. If you present ten points, the audience will decide the three they will remember and they are not likely to be the three you want them to remember. By selecting your three key points and clearly presenting them, you influence what they retain.

The Power of a Great Story

We coach technical teams that are making proposal presentations worth $100 million to a billion dollars. We have helped them win even when they were not the leading contender.

For example, government contracts frequently require those who will ultimately provide the service to present the oral portion of the proposal. Typically, technical professionals weren't trained to be presenters. They were trained to execute projects. Our challenge is to help them craft their message and delivery in a way that is memorable and persuasive.

One way we helped them do so is to teach them to switch seamlessly between data and stories. Even with a technically oriented government audience, the use of relevant personal stories makes a connection with the audience, which is remembered long after the details have been forgotten. Teams are often initially resistant to this concept, but they soon realize after seeing themselves on tape that sharing something other than data will make their presentation come to life. Using stories as examples, they can illustrate their depth of experience, their commitment to customer service and their cross-functional competence.

All the teams we have coached with this approach have won their contracts. If coupling data and stories can impress a government jury of assessors, it will absolutely work for your audience.

Stories are also powerful for corporate presentations. This concept was proven when we were coaching ten leaders from a global corporation in preparation for their annual international sales conference. Our goal with these executives was to ensure their presentations delivered the key messages in a way that complemented each other while providing a variety of styles.

Each presentation was built around a core personal story to help the audience authentically connect with the speaker. The stories were chosen to connect to the point of view of the customers and their sales force sitting in front of them.

The situation was complicated by one of the international leaders, Olaf. He was arriving very late from a hectic negotiation session in Moscow that had been prolonged. Our first chance to work with him was in the middle of the night, a mere 12 hours before his big presentation. Someone else had written Olaf's speech for him and it did not flow well. We had a big job ahead of us to make this speech work for Olaf in this timeframe.

Olaf's topic was teamwork. As we sat in the empty presentation hall that night, we began by asking him why he believed so strongly in teamwork and kept digging deeper until he told us an amazing story. To impress a young lady he was attracted to at the time, he joined a macho fishing boat crew in his native Norway at age 16.

Dangers of Nordic fishing include falling into icy cold, rough seas that can kill you in minutes. On his first trip out, the fish were spotted and the orders went out to man the smaller fishing boats. Olaf jumped from the larger boat to a smaller boat and fell into the ocean. To his amazement, the other team members did not hesitate to risk their lives by jumping into the frigid water to save him. That day never left his memory... and the crew never let him forget it!

We challenged Olaf to build his speech around that story. After looking at us as though we were insane, he finally agreed to take the risk. By sharing this part of himself, it allowed a wide group of highly influential people to see Olaf's humorous side, not just his stoic Norwegian bearing. He wove the story into his concept of international teamwork so beautifully that it became one of the most memorable presentations of the conference.

Olaf enhanced his standing in the company after that presentation because of his touch of vulnerability and humor, which greatly enhanced his perceived executive presence.

Prepare to Open and Close Memorably

The first 30 seconds and the last 30 seconds of your presentation can make or break the lasting impression. Take a risk in your opening and your closing to brand your message in the minds of the audience. Whatever you do, don't waste these precious opening seconds with something inane like, "It's a pleasure to be here today." Instead, open with something intriguing, interesting or startling, such as, "This technology is going to affect our business. If you ignore it, we'll be out of business."

Take a risk in your opening and your closing to brand your message in the minds of the audience.

One of our clients had no idea how powerfully an opening could affect perceptions. Mary was seen as a talented but reserved person who was a new Vice President with the company. She wasn't well known, so our goal was to get her known and remembered in the most positive possible light.

She was going to present at a conference where the theme was "Genuine Hospitality." We got her to open her first major conference presentation with her new company by playing the song, "There's No Place Like Home" on a harmonica! She was ready to kill us for talking her into the concept as she waited to go on stage, but it worked. After Mary was introduced, she began playing back stage. You could hear the music on the speakers but could not see her until she walked into a spotlight on the darkened stage. When she finished the song, there was a moment of silence and then she got a thunderous ovation—before she even started to speak!

Mary tied the music to the conference theme by describing how her father taught her to play the harmonica as a kid on warm summer evenings on their back step, linking that into a message on the importance of getting different departments to play effectively together like instruments in an orchestra. It took great courage on her part and excellent execution, but the people who saw that presentation talked about it for years. It significantly accelerated Mary's career in the organization.

In a less dramatic, but equally impactful manner, we were coaching Chris, a lead project manager, on the oral presentation for a proposal to run the data centers for a federal college loan program. We found out that this man had received a loan from this same program 25 years earlier. It was so important to him that he saved his acceptance letter for the student loan that he'd received as a senior in high school.

We asked Chris to tell this jaded, skeptical government audience the story behind the letter, the message of a kid with a single mother living in poverty who would have had absolutely no chance of attending college without that loan program. He opened his portion of the presentation with this story. Chris told his potential government customers who administered that same loan program how he understood what this funding meant to hundreds of thousands of potential students, because at one time, he had been one of those kids. He closed it with his personal commitment to do whatever it took to make the data delivery for this program work. His group won the contract based primarily on the strength of the presentation.

Change The Channel—Before They Do!

Prepare your message with variety that keeps the audience's attention. Even with a great opening, audience members are quick to let their thoughts wander to other things or get bored or disengage. We spend much of our time in coaching sessions giving people permission to be interesting to their audiences. Once you have the audience's attention, you need to work at keeping their attention. If you aren't having fun and being a little larger than you are in real life, your presentation is guaranteed to be forgettable for the audience. All audiences go through peaks and valleys of interest, no matter who is speaking to them. Showing executive presence and authenticity means rising above your fear factor and taking the risk to show something unique and interesting.

People's expectations are set by the fast-paced media world. Studies on remote control usage indicate that women will leave a television program on for about 15 seconds before changing the channel, but men only about 2 to 4 seconds! We once had a client who would put the radio in his rental cars on "scan," and leave it there the whole trip!

To counter the distractions, keep track of ideas, quotes, statistics and stories that support the key areas you want the audience to remember and use them to keep re-engaging your audience. You need to take the risk to show your audience a variety of delivery and interactive changes—speak softer, faster, louder, slower, show something, bring someone up front—do a wide variation of stimuli to keep bringing their attention back. Most importantly, take the risk to make a personal connection. One of our clients, Janet, did this brilliantly.

Janet was scheduled to present to the Board of Directors of her Fortune 500 company. Her objective was to convince them to withdraw a legacy food product that had been a part of the company for as long as anyone could remember. She knew that two prior attempts by her predecessors had both failed miserably, using just logic and facts.

One simplification test we use to make a message compelling and memorable is, "Would a 13-year-old understand your message?" It turned out that Janet had a son, Sean, that age, so she asked him what he thought would get the point across. Sean immediately said, "Mom, have they ever smelled that stuff?" That gave her the opening she needed.

On presentation day, Janet had the food product spread on crackers and placed on beautiful silver trays. At a predetermined cue, after five minutes of presenting the bottom-line data, the doors of the boardroom opened and several assistants brought in the trays. She asked each Board member to take just one cracker and taste it. The smell was so bad in the boardroom that they had to keep the doors open! By that afternoon, Janet had her decision to drop the product line. She took a risk, but given the history with the Board, Janet needed a message that was memorable, simple and effective. She got it—with Sean's help.

Once you have prepared your compelling message, you need to make sure to deliver the message powerfully.

Powerful Delivery

What do people spend most of their time on when preparing a presentation? Their visuals. Why? Because they can control them. Unfortunately, visuals tend to distract many presenters and distance them from their audiences.

One of our clients, Nic, had a presentation nightmare because of focusing on his PowerPoint slides and not on the conversation. Nic was scheduled to give a presentation to a senior executive at one of the top three US television networks. He assumed he needed to have the PowerPoint presentation of his life to address this highly sophisticated media expert.

Nic's stereotypes initially were confirmed when he was escorted into the boardroom. It looked like the bridge of the Starship Enterprise from the television show "Star Trek," with so many screens and control panels. He took a deep breath and cued up his computer to his slide show and waited for the entrance of his potential customer. The network executive walked in, graciously shook Nic's hand and introduced himself. Then he leaned over and pushed the power button of Nic's computer, turning it off. "No PowerPoint today, Nic," he said. "Just talk to me."

Nic was paralyzed for a moment; everything he'd so carefully planned had just been abandoned. After he recovered his composure, he swallowed hard and started to tell this prospective customer the story of their product and why it made sense for his network. Nic got the business. When Nic recounted this story to us, he said, "You know, despite my initial terror, I only forgot a couple of points—everything else just flowed because it became a conversation, not a presentation."

Do not let PowerPoint get in your way.

Presentations are about connecting with the audience. Do not let PowerPoint get in your way. Use PowerPoint visuals when they are essential. For the rest of the presentation consider turning the screen to black with no visual. You can do that with a black slide or you can press the "B" key on the keyboard. This places the audience's attention on you instead of your visuals and allows you to engage them with strong eye contact and powerful delivery.

Visual and Vocal Delivery

Our experience is that 95% of our clients need to use more variation in their delivery pattern, visually and vocally. Most people think their style is bigger than it really looks on the outside. There are exceptions, but for almost everyone, aligning the inside intention with the outside perception means expanding the comfort zone in presentations to really optimize effectiveness. They need to adjust their internal meters to authentically influence the audience.

Audiences judge a tremendous amount of your perceived commitment and passion based on two things: your vocal inflections and facial expressions. The good news is that by making relatively simple changes in delivery, you improve the appearance of confidence.

Your rate of speech helps you connect with your audience. We've seen many rapid, highly excitable talkers who are very hard to understand. *Theygoveryquicklywithnopausesatall!* They can confuse the audience and can be exhausting to listen to. Conversely, most audiences get impatient with speakers who are overly deliberate or too slow in their pace.

There are definite geographic differences in the rate of speech. In a Midwestern city like Minneapolis, the average speaking rate is about 125 words per minute. In parts of New York, Boston or Philadelphia, the average rate can be closer to 225 words per minute. In the Midwest, a "fast talker" is not to be trusted. Conversely, it is common for a New Yorker to think the "slow talker" is less intelligent or naive. Bringing your vocal rate closer to the rate of your audience can make a tremendous difference in your perceived executive presence.

Slowing down the pace of your speech at key moments makes you seem more confident, competent, thoughtful, relaxed and in control. By contrast, speeding up your rate for brief moments of motivation or excitement gives an energy boost to your audience.

One of our British clients did not realize how fast he was talking. When we made a video recording, he couldn't understand what he'd said when we played it back! On top of that, he was dealing with audiences who had English as their second or even third language. Just learning to adjust his rate of speed 25% slower created a dramatic increase in his effectiveness.

Pause and Punch

To really show poise, presence and create dynamic impact, nothing beats a pause. If you pause in the middle of a sentence, the listener will focus more on what you're saying. Think about how announcers always put a big pause in the middle of what they're saying. It hooks you in as you wait with bated breath to hear what comes after the pause. When you hear, "And the winner of the one million dollar prize is..." you won't turn the channel until you hear what comes after the pause!

John Kennedy, Martin Luther King, Jr. and Winston Churchill were masters of the pause for emphasis. Churchill was especially good at this because he spoke for a radio audience and was a severe stutterer. His "pause and punch" technique kept him from stuttering. He would underline words he wanted to emphasize on his text and placed slash marks at pause points. Kennedy borrowed this technique from Churchill and had the same kind of powerful impact with a television audience. The following example, from JFK's inaugural address, is first written in a traditional paragraph style:

John Kennedy, Martin Luther King, Jr. and Winston Churchill were masters of the pause for emphasis.

"Ask not what your country can do for you; ask what you can do for your country."

When you see Kennedy's hand-written notes at the JFK Library in Massachusetts, you see that the words are organized by phrase, using an underline for a punch and a slash for a pause, based on how they would sound to the listener. They look like this:

Ask <u>not</u> /

what your <u>country</u> can do

for <u>you</u> ///

ask what <u>you</u> can do /

for

your

country.

Think about when you could selectively use this approach to increase the emphasis of your key statement in your presentation. Your presentations will be more powerful when you courageously deliver your content with pause and punch.

Warm-up

When Carol worked at The Guthrie Theater, she would watch the actors warm up before a presentation. Depending on the complexity of the role, they took up to 90 minutes to get their bodies ready for the role they were going to play—before they even put on a costume or makeup! Your body is an important part of your presentation. Don't take your body for granted. Breathing and stretching can save your body from betraying you in a presentation. Use the same breathing and stretching exercises discussed in Chapter Three to prepare your body to deliver a powerful message.

Your Hands

The most common question we hear regarding the visual aspect of presentations is, "What do I do with my hands?" The answer is to move them with intent. Without intent, hands move randomly when you're nervous, which is distracting to the audience.

Develop the ability to "hold" a gesture, to hold a pause and to show steady eye contact to convey your commitment.

For many people, gestures are a natural part of everyday conversation, but when they get in front of an audience, they are not sure what to do. In general, the gestures should be natural and bigger for larger groups. Keep your hands apart when speaking. Most people unconsciously show their nervousness when their hands clench, tightly clasp each other or play with a pen or pointer.

During your presentation, try a wider variety of stronger, firmer, broader gestures, such as:

- The determined confidence of holding one fist anywhere in front of you and punching it for emphasis of your words.
- Holding your arms out with your palms up to display inclusiveness or sincerity.
- A comparison gesture with one hand out to one side, then the other hand out to the other side.

Bigger gestures generally mean raising your arms away from your body so there is more "air in your armpits." Remember, you're painting pictures with your hands to help the audience come along with you, so make it a billboard, not a postage stamp. Doing so will help you increase your range as a speaker.

Audiences Expect to be Entertained

Audiences today expect to be entertained. They are waiting for you to be interesting. Make no mistake about it—you are an actor in that particular medium called the corporate presentation.

Every presentation is a performance. In any performance, you need deliver much more than content. If you're just going to read your notes to the audience, or make your PowerPoint slides your speech, you're better off sending your audience the content and saving everyone some time. They can read it faster than you can deliver it and you won't bore them, but you also won't connect with them.

Actors know that they have to grab the audience immediately. They do this by starting at what they call "the top of the scene," meaning that their energy level must connect them to the audience right from their entrance. In a similar manner, your opening is crucial. Your first two minutes should make audience members glad they took the time to be there. If you wait to prove relevance, you've lost a lot of ground.

You need to read the audience's energy level and start with a somewhat higher energy than the audience has. One place to do so is in how you interact physically. We discussed facial expression in detail during Chapter Three, so just remember one critical thing for a presentation—inform your face that you're happy to be there! Lighten up. Even though public speaking is the number-one most-feared activity for many people, you need to let your face capitalize on this opportunity. If your face is flat and disengaged, your audience will be as well.

No audience wants the speaker to look nervous, because it makes them very uncomfortable. They want you to take control of the room immediately. Making solid eye contact gives a sense of executive presence.

Let the audience see your eyes. If you're not committed to your message, why should they be? When you look at just one person in your audience, five people in the cluster around them feel that you are looking at them as well. Address a single individual, make eye contact, hold it steadily for a few seconds, then move on to someone else. It's a great way to connect with your audience in order to get movement and commitment.

How many presenters have you seen nervously moving back and forth, pacing like caged animals? One of the biggest problems we see, even when coaching top executives, is that many either move impetuously or they lock their knees up and freeze in a strangely contorted position. We once had to grab the ankles of a company president, in a private coaching session, to keep him from rapidly moving from side to side as he spoke. The look on his face was priceless, but every time he was tempted to wander from then on, he remembered that moment!

No audience wants the speaker to look nervous, because it makes them very uncomfortable.

Keep your lower body still, but loose. Put your feet about shoulder-width apart. Widen your stance for stability and soften how tightly you hold your knees. It keeps you far more stable when you're tense. When you move, make sure that your movement is purposefully emphasizing your content. If you want to take one step, go at least three steps in that direction and stop. Commit to the movement strongly. Make a note on your script where it makes logical sense to move. Make your point, pause, move, and then make your next point.

Gestures, eye contact and a wider stance will feel odd at first, but they won't look strange to your audience. They'll just give you solid, authentic executive presence as a presenter.

Panel Discussion

If you're doing a panel or a group presentation, eye contact can help you win the crowd over by showing active team engagement. This is critical, because you're being judged not just on what you say, but on how the team interacts. We work with many team presenters and they are consistently stunned to see how bored they look when their partners are speaking! We ask them to show an active team attitude in this way:

- Show your team members eye contact, encouragement, energy and engagement. If you don't seem interested, why should your audience?
- Even when something goes awry with one of your team members, don't let it throw you—stay relaxed visually.

Let the way you engage with your audience and your team make believers out of your audience.

Make It Real

We close this chapter on Audience Connection with a story about a man who grew tremendously in this arena. Dave Hubers had just been promoted from CFO to CEO of what was then American Express Financial Advisors. We were coaching him for his inaugural address to the company, which was being simulcast across the country to all their satellite locations. Dave was an extremely intelligent, introverted leader with great integrity and humility.

The first draft of Dave's speech was a statistics-laden, fact-heavy presentation that told us absolutely nothing about his personality or his beliefs. We thought it was crucial for Dave to quickly establish his human side to the company in this presentation since virtually everyone already trusted him on the analytical side. What they needed to know was his passion and his heart.

After hearing his first run-through, we said to him, "Dave, you have to talk about your arm." Dave was clearly startled by this statement. Dave had lost his right arm in a car accident when he was 18 years old and had worn a prosthesis for some 35 years. He took his prosthesis for granted because it had been part of him for longer than he'd had his real arm. He asked, "What about my arm?" We explained, "People don't know how to shake your hand. They don't know if it is OK to look at your arm."

This blew him away, so we went on to tell him, "Dave, this is a chance to tell them your story of a bright, athletic kid from a little town in rural Minnesota who lost his arm as a high school senior when he was the captain of the basketball team. It's the story of the young man who lost his college athletic scholarship and seemingly all his chances for success. Tell them how this experience impacted you; how it redirected you; how it made you the man you are today and the leader you'll be for them tomorrow."

During a long, long pause, we thought Dave was going to get up, walk away and call the whole thing off. After all, he was an extremely private and powerful man who was used to taking total accountability for his actions. He was not used to being vulnerable. However, slowly, Dave decided that what we were saying might make some sense. He courageously stood on that stage in front of the cameras and the live audience and as part of his presentation, he told his story.

Dave told his people about how devastated he was by the amputation of his right arm and the loss of his dreams to play college basketball, but how it had positively refocused his energy to a completely different direction, that of finance and accounting. His drive and determination to function with one arm never left him and that's what allowed him to become CEO of the same company he'd joined when he graduated from college. He talked about overcoming obstacles and hanging through in tough times. He ended by telling them to feel free to just grab his left hand when they wanted to greet him.

No one ever forgot that presentation. Dave didn't, either. He told us, after the experience was over, "I realized that I was showing too much credibility and not enough personality!" When Dave retired some years later, he was stunned by how many people came up to tell him how that speech was one of the reasons they decided to hang in with the company during some difficult times. That presentation memorably influenced them and their feelings about the company long after he was gone. What a wonderful legacy to leave behind by demonstrating authentic executive presence in a high-integrity manner. It pays to see yourself as others do.

C OMMAND

L EVERAGE

E XPECTATIONS

A UDIENCE

R ELATIONSHIP

L ISTENING

I NSPIRATION

7

RELATIONSHIP COMPETENCE, LOCALLY AND REMOTELY

Interpersonal skills have always been key to leadership success, but their importance has been increased by globalization, instantaneous communications and the expectation of 24/7 electronic interactions. The speed and access to communication has changed how we lead around the world, in different buildings or across the table. We are all dependent on so many people to get our jobs done today. Relationship competence can make or break your effectiveness locally and globally at all stages of your career.

Knowing How Others See You Around the World

Many people have not given much thought to how they're perceived when they communicate electronically. Despite relying so heavily on this medium because of its convenience, its very speed can break down collaboration in the blink of an eye.

One of our European clients from Procter and Gamble provided a great synopsis of how to rebuild collaboration in remote relationships. She was highly regarded but had previously struggled with being seen as too independent. Independence was an attribute that had served her well earlier in her career, as she proved to her aggressive male constituents that she "had what it took" to succeed.

With her promotion, the same attribute was now proving to be problematic. In her new role, she needed to achieve consensus across many constituencies; groups with different geographies, agendas and nationalities.

After reading her data and watching herself on video, she said, "It's clear that I need to do some things very differently to be more collaborative. First, I need to show more respect. I need to acknowledge that my peers and subordinates are talented. I need to seek their advice and align in advance with my peers on the direction I want to take, to show more clearly that I care about their opinions.

"Even if I don't particularly like them, I have to respect that they are contacts for certain functions I may need in the future, so I can't leave them out of the loop, even on small details that could cause them to lose face. I need to advise them in advance on what I'm expecting them to do in order to get the ball to move forward—don't surprise them or they'll surprise me in the future when I least expect it and when I need them most."

As this client learned, it's important to build relationships to get results. This is even truer if you want effective remote communications.

Remote Communication Effectiveness

How remote you are when you communicate is all a matter of degree. It might have nothing to do with physical distance. We've seen people have a cool, distant relationship working in an office next door while working well with team members in Boston and Singapore! It doesn't matter if you're in New York and your people are in Texas, or if you're in Europe and your people are scattered across the globe, leadership communication on a remote level has unique challenges that require a certain type of attention.

Even putting a department on two different floors significantly decreases communication, so imagine what it's like to be separated by two continents, with an ocean and eight time zones between you! But maybe you're not working across the globe—maybe you're just moving to a different part of the building.

As challenging as it can be to effectively communicate face-to-face, it is significantly more difficult when the other person is remote, whether in a different building or on a different continent. It's exhausting when you are communicating with team members, colleagues or leaders in every time zone, as some of our clients are doing today. We have conducted surveys on this topic that support what you might have experienced—that you need to be even more explicit, in a warmer manner, when working virtually because of all the missing face-to-face cues.

Even putting a department on two different floors significantly decreases communication, so imagine what it's like to be separated by two continents, with an ocean and eight time zones between you!

Remote communication will continue to expand as more people work at home, offsite or around the globe. We are highly dependent on the use of electronic tools as a significant portion of our communication capability. These tools can have an immediate positive impact on organizational results and performance, but they can also make life miserable for many people because of the lack of thought given to the way we use them.

Earlier in the book, we identified that the total communication impact of visual, vocal and content shows how content is a small part of your initial communication effectiveness. Most electronic communication focuses on content, minimizing or eliminating the significant visual and vocal portion of communication, which contributes significantly to accurate interpretation. No wonder there are so many misunderstandings when using electronic communication devices.

One-on-one, in-person meetings have the highest potential for communicating accurate intent because the visual, vocal and content aspects are all apparent. Despite this, you know how open to confusion even one-on-one communication can be. Electronic modalities are even more prone to misinterpretation.

A poorly written e-mail or text mail is as likely to miscommunicate as to communicate the intended message. We'll describe the impact of "e-missiles" later in this chapter. A conference call has content and vocal impact, so there is more potential for accurate communication. However, conference calls are limited in terms of their ability to read the intended context from participants if the transmission is choppy with awkward pauses or gaps. It's also hard to maintain interest in a conference call or video conference, so people check out rapidly unless there are deliberate approaches to keep people engaged. We have some of these techniques on our website for further exploration: SeeingYourselfAsOthersDo.com/reference.

> **Recent research has found that your impact on the phone is interpreted based 86% on the sound of the voice and a mere 14% on content.**

A one-on-one phone call moves up the potential for accurate communication because both parties have content and vocal communications to attempt to convey their intent, but they can't read your eyes or your face. So, you have to really make your message clear through your voice. Recent research has found that your impact on the phone is interpreted based 86% on the sound of the voice and a mere 14% on content.

A web-based meeting helps create visual representation of content that is clearer and allows for visual confirmation of collaboration. This can add efficacy to the communications, but it has limited value to communicate the emotions or passion about a topic.

Videoconferencing adds a limited amount of visual impact, depending on the quality of the transmission and the number of people in the room who can be on camera.

Interestingly, with all the speed of electronic communications, a handwritten note has a charmingly quaint feel to it these days. Its permanence stands out in contrast to the transitory nature of digital print on a screen. What was the last handwritten note you received? How much do you remember about it? It tends to be retained and much more effective as a connection vehicle than an e-mail, text mail or even a voicemail. Try taking a few moments to do a handwritten thank-you note as a different way to provide a memorable, personal touch point.

Change Masters Remote Communication Survey Results

Who trained you to be more compassionate, engaging or warmly received electronically? No one, if you're like most people. You just received these new communication tools and were taught how to file or delete messages, not how to connect with others in this cool medium.

With this in mind, we surveyed 350 of our clients and their sponsors in 25 different companies to hear about their struggles and successes with remote communications. We asked about their real-life experiences with the challenges of making remote communication work and who did it best. It was clear that while everyone loved aspects of these communication technologies we've come to take for granted, their frustration with them was equally strong. This topic clearly touched a nerve with people, based on the number of responses we received and the vehemence people expressed.

The top three findings on effective remote communications were as follows:

- 52% said that people would say things electronically that they'd never say face-to-face.
- 70% said that due to the less personal nature of electronic communications, false assumptions could be made around comprehension or understanding.

- 71% said that they are literally forgetting people who are "out of sight, out of mind."

Think of the significance of over half the people around you being willing to be rude electronically in a way they'd never consider doing face-to-face. When compounded with the fact that over two-thirds of the time you could be misinterpreted electronically, clearly a communication conundrum exists.

There were a number of issues with electronic messages we gleaned from the Remote Communications Survey:

1. Their impersonal nature
2. The sheer volume of electronic messages
3. The content of electronic messages—grammatically incorrect, missing words, rambling nature, juvenile abbreviations
4. Indiscriminate distribution of electronic messages, cc'd to the world
5. Electronic media are cold and used for the wrong purposes
6. Time zone issues
7. Technical problems with teleconference/video conferencing

The consistent message in these issues was the lack of warmth and an abundance of frustration created by our incredibly necessary electronic communications tools. However, this can be countered. Everyone in our survey had seen excellent remote communicators who are time-effective, frequent and caring. None of their approaches were complicated, but they all made good common sense.

Best Practices in Remote Communications

A client who worked in a fully virtual setting realized at the end of his coaching, "The older I get, the more I understand that creating relationships is about the most important thing we do as leaders."

This gentleman understood the best practices that were suggested from our survey of remote communications.

The most powerful and consistent message was about the informal communications with people at other locations. Building and maintaining the personal relationships remotely were the greatest opportunities seen by the survey respondents. When people are at the same location, there are the inevitable informal conversations in the hallway, getting together over coffee, lunch or office birthday parties. When people are remote they often feel forgotten and left out of such connection activities. Most remote interactions are transactional rather than personal.

It became a huge priority for me to make relationships happen with subordinates who are here and abroad. Even though I don't have any more time than I did before, I take the time to see, call or e-mail every single one of my direct reports every day.

The best remote communicators spend face-to-face time early on in the relationship to build an emotional bank account that allows electronic communications to be more effective over time. They also take time to talk on the phone or electronically about what was going on in their lives similar to hallway or lunch conversations.

One person described a senior project leader, Chuck, as an outstanding remote communicator. Chuck led global teams in eight countries spread over three continents. Chuck had told him, "When I deal with that many time zones, I'm always behind in communicating with somebody. Each member of my group assumed that I was providing dramatically more leadership to everyone else. It's like having eight kids instead of two—the goal isn't equity any more; it's just about keeping your head above water as best as you can.

"It became a huge priority for me to make relationships happen with subordinates who are here and abroad. Even though I don't have any more time than I did before, I take the time to see, call or e-mail every single one of my direct reports every day.

"I 'go to lunch' with them in their time zone on the phone—we both eat and talk at their lunch times. I drop people an informal line, I talk to them about their lives, and I laugh with them about their kids' stories. They had better know why we're doing this versus that. I know now that you have to over-communicate, to make sure everyone is involved when working across time zones. It means you have to make communication a priority.

"You have to travel a lot early in a relationship and spend far more time on the phone when the groups get formed. This allows me to set the tone and culture. Relationships over the phone, video-conference or e-mail are much stronger if there is a face-to-face link established early on, even if it's just once."

Here are the best practice comments from our respondents in our Remote Communications Survey about how to be most successful when leading and communicating remotely:

1. When I'm working remotely myself, I do customized communication with the key people in the home office and I cycle through each person routinely to make sure I'm connecting with each one. I had to increase the time I spent communicating with them. Before, I had kept communications very infrequent, on a "need to know" basis to maximize the efficiency—so I was missing opportunities to influence them now that I was remote. I've learned that by focusing too much on efficiency, I minimized relationships with my centers of influence. That's not a good thing.

2. Great remote leadership is a combination of soft and hard skills. You don't really know what's happening, so you need to have a good infrastructure, such as ensuring that solid, consistent reporting processes are in place.

3. It's very important to build soft skills, to build a relationship so they feel you are their facilitator and champion. It's easy to feel like you're out there alone when you're remote, so you have to "feed" people in a more creative way. We place photographs of off-site employees on the wall. We've done fun things to connect the remote team with our local group, like sharing odd foods indigenous to the area they're in. I actually ate a fried cricket on a dare and my people loved it!

4. Think of what you're focusing on in the actual minutes of contact you have when you are face-to-face. If they represent a bad experience with someone you won't see for three months, then you're just being careless and thoughtless. You need to be aware of your impact and handle it accordingly, because those few minutes with you will change their productivity for a whole year.

5. I've learned that there's a validity to just connecting with people for the sake of connecting, and it's true up and down when you're the one who's an ex-pat—don't be overly concerned that you're not being appropriate by initiating contact with senior leaders you don't see as often. Respond quickly to voicemails and emails so they don't assume lack of interest.

6. I make myself available at pre-assigned contact hours that are during their workday and make use of many software and electronic communication tools that I had never used before. It's less warm in terms of media impact, however, so I also make a point to send them foods from home that I know they like. I've also had celebrations in our office in the States in recognition of their national traditions, taken pictures, and sent them back to our colleagues in other parts of the world. Use electronic communications to build relationships like you might have a hallway conversation if you were face-to-face.

7. Stan is my example of someone who really knows how to communicate effectively on a remote basis. It's almost like he's psychic—he just seems to know the exact moment to touch base with me. He drops me a two-line e-mail or a 15-second voicemail when I've just had my worst day in months. It strikes the perfect chord of support and a kick in the rear!

You're busy, you're overloaded already, but it doesn't have to take a lot of time to be a world-class best-practice remote relationship builder. It just takes awareness and a choice to stay connected in order to keep relationships intact, even in the most remote relationships you've got.

Eliminating E-missiles

The most used and most maligned remote communication tools are e-mail and text messages. They are very powerful tools and yet so many use them poorly. They work very well for time-shifting primarily short content-based information. They don't work well at all for communicating emotions or humor.

A joint study from the University of Chicago and New York University found that when participants were sent two groups of e-mails, one group meant to be sarcastic and one group meant to be sincere, the recipients misinterpreted the tone of the message 50 percent of the time, incorrectly identifying sarcastic messages as being not humorous but intentionally malicious. Imagine what perceptions that could create when you won't see the other person for six months!

We have developed ten rules for e-mail that address most of the issues and provide the opportunity to harvest the most from this medium.

Relationships and interpersonal communications continue to be key to leadership effectiveness both remotely and locally. The level of business intensity, globalization and electronic explosion will change forever the approach needed to demonstrate authentic executive

144

presence. Go to SeeingYourselfAsOthersDo.com/reference for more information on electronic communication best practices.

Where Workplace Relationships Go Awry

There are many elements to keeping workplace relationships strong and productive, whether locally or remotely. We will touch on three we find most often need to be brought to our clients' attention: meetings, trust and conflict.

One helpful metaphor for relationships is the emotional bank account, popularized by Stephen Covey. If we have a positive relationship, we make deposits into the emotional bank account and increase the strength of the relationship. When the emotional bank account is high, we tend to have more trust, so if there are several ways to interpret a statement or action, it is likely that one of the more positive interpretations will be selected.

Many times the deposits or withdrawals you make to or from your emotional bank account with others will be based on how you say something more than what you say.

However, broken promises, disrespect and unresolved conflict are withdrawals from the emotional bank account. When the balance goes below zero the relationship breaks down. In this situation the statements or actions will be interpreted in more negative terms and probably further withdraw from the emotional bank account.

For example, a couple in love, strolling down a garden path may actually say the opposite of what they mean, but they will laughingly interpret the message lovingly and openly. The same two people, years later in divorce court, might interpret a similar miscommunication in a very negative way because the emotional bank account has been deeply overdrawn.

Many times the deposits or withdrawals you make to or from your emotional bank account with others will be based on how you say something more than what you say. It might be the tone of voice or the facial expression you use. There might also have been experiences where trust has broken down for legitimate reasons. Often, when we meet clients with trust issues they do not even know what they have done to create a negative relationship.

In the last chapter of this book, we will expand on ways to make deposits to the emotional bank account. In this chapter, we will look at the day-to-day interactions that make adjustments to the account.

Meeting Basics That Make a Difference

One of the key areas of relationship influence and executive presence is in meetings both local and remote. Meetings have great potential to provide leadership, enroll people in the shared vision and organize efforts to maximize the effectiveness of the group. Dramatic results can be achieved in a great meeting.

Unfortunately, most meetings are viewed as a waste of time by the participants. Ask anyone, "How effective are the meetings in your organization?" You're likely to hear a ten-minute rant on how many meetings there are, how worthless they are, and how it keeps people from getting "real work" done. *Meeting Magazine* reported that only 5% of all meetings are rated as having meaningful dialogue that reaches decisions on important issues.

3M reported that an average meeting costs about $15,000 an hour. It is not hard to believe. For your organization, calculate the ratio of salary to the total sales. Take that ratio times two to calculate your meeting factor (MF). For each person in the meeting, take their average salary per hour times the MF to calculate a conservative estimate per hour. Add travel time and expenses and it is not hard to come up with a $15,000 meeting.

There are many examples of bad meetings and even more examples of too many meetings. Lack of preparation becomes a vicious cycle that wastes time and causes more meetings so there is less time to prepare. Political situations often make it necessary to be at meetings to know what is going on even if it is not very much. People go to meetings in resistance rather than to create results.

When participating in meetings, use them to demonstrate your professionalism, your acumen and your executive presence. How you engage in them makes a big difference in how you're perceived. One way to stand out as having executive presence is to run really effective meetings. This can differentiate you from others in a very positive way. We have seen people improve their reputations by running tight, professional meetings that are relevant, productive and fun.

One way to stand out as having executive presence is to run really effective meetings.

Your clarity in meetings, whether in-person or electronic, is noticed. Often, meetings are the only direct data point your peers and other leaders have about you. They contribute greatly to you being perceived as a clear thinker. To let those around you know that, you need to participate in meetings so people know where you stand, but avoid talking just to hear yourself talk.

Meeting Basics

You can decide to have excellent meetings. Even in an environment where meetings are poorly run, you can be the exception. The following guidelines are meeting fundamentals, which can help you display executive presence. They're common principles that are constantly violated.

1. Be clear about the purpose of the meeting, even if it is a routine team meeting. Ask if there is a better way to achieve the objective than having a meeting. If it is a regular meeting, can you do it half as often and be just as effective?

2. Only invite those who can bring value or have a need to know, and be clear about your expectations.

3. Have a timed agenda distributed well in advance of the meeting. If people only need participate for a small segment of the agenda, let them come and go for their time slot. Indicate the agenda item is for decision, discussion or feedback.

4. Start and end on time (or early if possible). We know a Vice President who locked the door at the start time of his staff meetings. Anyone who was not there was not able to attend. He only had to do this a few times to make the message clear. Start on time even if not everyone is present, because it is respectful to those who do arrive on time.

5. Be clear why each person attends and be clear about his or her role. Even if higher-level people are in the meeting, remember you are running the meeting.

6. Stick to the agenda, but promote discussion and debate.

7. Bring each point to conclusion, and document the conclusion. If there are follow-up actions, be sure the responsibilities are clear and accepted in the meeting by someone who is in the meeting. If the action is for someone not in attendance, someone present in the meeting should have that action until it is accepted by someone else.

8. Make the meeting interesting. Bring in food, show a movie clip to illustrate your concept, read an e-mail from a satisfied customer. Break up the routine positively.

9. Send out minutes with the action items to the meeting participants. Copy those that have a need to know and were not at the meeting.

10. Seek feedback from participants on how future meetings could be improved.

Participating In Meetings with Executive Presence

If you are a participant invited to a meeting, you can ask the organizer about the purpose and your role in the meeting if they have not already offered that information.

Be a role model for being prepared and engaged in the meeting by doing the following:

- Know what you want to achieve in the meeting.
- Monitor your talk-time to see that you are participating enough without talking too much.
- Pick your battles.
- Continually look at the OPPOV being demonstrated by the other participants.
- Be as authentically supportive of others in the meeting as possible.

Be a role model for being prepared and engaged in the meeting

In relation to the last point, here's a question we get all the time: "What should I do when an idea I throw out on the table is not accepted and a few days later someone else suggests my idea? The group jumps on it and gives that person credit. How do I maintain my poise and still manage to get acknowledged for my contribution when a peer is ripping off my idea?"

The manner in which you deliver the message and how well you tie it back to what others are concerned about make all the difference. It's important not to take this slight personally. Most groups have very short memories for who said what. In the crush of doing business today, if you just bring up an idea once, or say it quickly without much energy, others probably won't recognize you for it. So rather than get mad and pout or feel slighted and plot your revenge, get engaged!

Immediately bridge what was just said by others to your idea with comments like, "I completely agree with what Jim is saying. It's completely in line with what I spoke about in our last meeting, when I talked about creating a strategy where we get that information in advance." This way you subtly remind others that you were the one who had brought it up in the first place.

Trust—Remote and Local

Locally or globally, we have all needed to work with people we don't understand, or maybe even dislike. There are also people who have interests that you don't share. Business relationships do not have all the same requirements that personal relationships do. It is helpful if you personally like many of the people you work with, but it's not always going to happen. Don't try to get your emotional needs met at the office.

One of the keys to relationships is trust.

It is essential, however, to be respectful, interested in the other person, and trustworthy to build relationships and maintain them. Here's how a highly respected senior female executive put it when she worked with a number of men who were into sports. She said, "I need to work the informal network side. You don't have to be a sports nut to do so. I never read *Sports Illustrated* and I've survived. I just show some interest in their banter. I don't withdraw but I don't fake knowing something about sports. Instead, I made it a point to know about their college visits with their kids and draw them out on those topics. It is an authentic interest for me and it builds relationships with them."

One of the keys to relationships is trust. We talked about it in the area of politics, but it is tied to emotional bank accounts and has additional aspects as well. When people talk about trust they will often say, "I am trusting until they prove me wrong." Almost everyone who makes that binary proclamation admits just about everyone lets him or her down at some point. It's a steep fall from grace and tough to recover once they trip.

A more helpful way to look at trust is as a scaled matrix. The horizontal side of the matrix lists different areas of trust, such as being on time, telling the truth, delivering what they commit to do, keeping confidences and taking accountability. The vertical side of the matrix is a scale from one to ten that indicates your amount of trust in each area. You might give a high trust score to someone for delivering on time, but give them a low trust score in terms of keeping confidences.

A good place to start with people is to set all the ratings at five and then base your trust on how they behave. As they prove worthy of trust in an area, the score goes up. When they are continually late to meetings, your trust in that area goes down. This approach helps avoid the black-and-white thinking on trust perceptions that gets many people in trouble and breaks down relationships both locally and remotely.

Broken trust in workplace relationships is one of the trickiest areas we face with clients. When we write survey questions, by far the toughest one for our clients is "Do you trust Joe? Why or why not?"

The first words out of the mouth of any client who gets critical feedback on this question are remarkably similar. They sound something like, "But I always do what I say I will do—why wouldn't they trust me?" They immediately jump to an extreme, feeling like they're being called a liar or having their character called into question if there's any critical input on trust.

Well, you can get everything done on time and still not be trusted. Why? As we said in our chapter on leveraging influence and power, it's because trust isn't just about prompt task completion. In reality, trust is a very complex balance of a number of different things. Harvard Management Review says, in their September 2000 issue, "Trust may be just as important a determinant of economic prosperity as physical capital, if only because it allows people in organizations to work together more effectively. But trust isn't exactly something you can buy off the shelf."

Seeing yourself as others do will be of great benefit in understanding relationships because people trust you or do not trust you based on their perception and not on your internal intent. Misunderstandings and misperceptions cause a cycle of mistrust to be created and perpetuated. We have helped many clients dramatically improve trust relationships with key people in their lives.

Rebuilding trust is never an overnight process. You can't talk your way out of a situation you have behaved your way into. New behaviors take time to be believed. When our clients commit to rebuilding trust in an organization, it takes 6–18 months for people to really believe they'll stick to their new behaviors.

Rebuilding Broken Trust

Trust is even more challenging to regain in a group than with a single person. If you have a strong emotional bank account with a group, people will more likely give you the benefit of the doubt in your communications. However, if you have an emotional bank account that is in deficit, others can quickly jump to the conclusion that you're just out for yourself or have some other self-serving, negative intention.

Sometimes the emotional bank account is based on your role and not you personally. This was the experience of Derek, who was the new Vice President of Human Resources for a national health-care services organization.

During his first month on the job, Derek met with a field service group he had inherited as part of his responsibilities. The people in this room had felt ignored for years. Derek instantly sensed the hostility in the room. They were ready for battle with the enemy from corporate.

Derek scrapped his plans to just say hello for five minutes and move on because the sales managers started vigorously and bitterly complaining to him about the lack of service support they were receiving. They were justified in their anger. The call abandonment rate was excessive, because it was taking the call center representatives twelve minutes to answer customer calls!

Derek immediately moved to sincerely listening. He asked the group to take fifteen minutes and list every question and complaint. He told them he'd leave the room so they could be candid. When he returned, he committed to answer each and every question to the best of his ability and committed to present the other questions to his senior leaders.

When they finished with their laundry lists of complaints, the group was dramatically calmer. They'd had a chance to discuss the issues without feeling judged by the Home Office. Derek said, "Look, I know Field Services is broken. I know you're frustrated with the level of service you've been receiving. It's clear we've made a lot of mistakes. There's no question. We all have."

That's when Derek demonstrated a great moment of executive presence. He chose to show empathy by being personally vulnerable with the group by sharing his own story. He told them, "We have all made mistakes. My biggest mistake was to allow my ex-wife to take my toddlers with her and live half a world away. For a long time, I was a victim. I blamed her. I was so angry. My life didn't get any better until I took accountability and worked out a way to get with my kids again.

"We all have a choice to be victims or to be accountable. I've been a victim in the past, and I don't ever want to go there again. We've all made mistakes—we're all accountable. I commit to giving 100 percent to help us be accountable to each other. I ask that you do the same."

There was a pause, which seemed endless, followed by a standing ovation from this jaded, frustrated group of remote managers! Based on their input, the call center staffing was changed so the call abandonment rate dropped dramatically.

Derek took the risk to be vulnerable, open and to listen to the needs of others in a remote situation where there were a lot of pent-up needs. He earned their trust because he provided a dramatically different approach than the group had experienced before.

Cycles of Mistrust

Derek had the advantage of being new, which allowed the group to believe that things would be different going forward. More often the trust needs to rebuilt when there is a history of mistrust with two parties or two groups.

Looking at how you perceive the other person and how they perceive you in an objective manner helps you get off the gerbil wheel of the cycle of mistrust.

Understanding how the cycle of mistrust perpetuates itself requires one person in the cycle to make the mature decision to change behaviors and show authentic executive presence. If you want to change the cycle of mistrust with someone, the first step is to understand how your behavior is contributing to the mistrust. Looking at how you perceive the other person and how they perceive you in an objective manner helps you get off the gerbil wheel of the cycle of mistrust. By changing a few key factors of behavior, you can have a significant impact on the reactions of the other person. In some cases, this awareness can even shift a broken relationship to a cycle of trust. More information on this concept of changing cycles of mistrust is available at: SeeingYourselfAsOthersDo.com/reference.

Healthy Conflict

The final element to keeping workplace relationships strong and productive is conflict, whether remote or local. Healthy conflict is important in organizations to build ideas, resolve competing priorities and make progress. Avoiding conflict undermines the opportunities for healthy relationships in organizations.

Conflict situations are often emotional as well as factual. As a result, the medium in which you resolve it if you're remote is crucial in order to not be misperceived. Go for the best source of connection you can when dealing with conflict. Pick up the phone if you can't get face-to-face.

Our observation after twenty-five years of coaching is that when conflict is not healthy, the average emotional age of the workplace deteriorates to around 13 years old. Think of a seventh-grade lunchroom and the dynamics in place there. Seventh graders are not great at conflict resolution, and some adults get stuck at this stage, never progressing beyond this point emotionally. Their feelings are easily hurt, they form coalitions, they tell you one thing and do another or they squabble so much that an authority figure needs to step in and make a decision. This is not good for the organization or for the individuals.

Strong leaders with executive presence focus on the higher-level goals that unite all of the parties and help them work through conflict constructively. Sometimes, patience is all it takes to deal with challenging relationships. Take Joe, a client we first met many years ago who later became the CEO of his Fortune 500 company. Back when we were coaching him, he was dealing with a work relationship that was causing him a great deal of frustration. He was going through all sorts of machinations on what he should do about this person in his coaching session when Carol said to him, "Joe, this guy has a high ego and low self-esteem. Just wait him out. He's going to self-destruct." And he did.

Dealing with Conflict Among Groups

Tom Debrowski, Executive Vice President of Operations of Mattel, has been successful at three global organizations. He shared his perspective on conflict in three very different cultures by saying, "Sometimes you're dealing with other departments who are hostile to you or your team. In many organizations, one department's success is perceived as being at the cost of someone else's department.

"You need to change that perception or you'll hear something like, 'Well, the Operations guys did a great job of saving money but their service levels stunk—they didn't get the product to us because they didn't want to ship less than a full truckload, and it was three days late.' With that perception, all of the sales people hate operations! They think all you care about is getting your costs down and that will make you a hero, but in the meantime, they have customers yelling at them because they're not getting product! Their thinking is, 'You don't understand what I have to live with when Wal-Mart is breathing down my neck!'

"Whenever there is a gap between two groups in a company, it's usually because the top people never sat down face-to-face to talk openly and honestly, so all kinds of nasty things can happen at levels below them. When they do meet, they find out you're not that far apart, or if you are, it doesn't take much to resolve things quickly. Leaders need to tell their people that they won't tolerate inappropriate cross-department behavior and explain what we are working toward together. Then just like that, the issue goes away."

Leading Your Former Peers

Tom Debrowski also gave us his perspective on another area that can damage relationships: the touchy issue of being promoted above your former peers. He noted, "It is awkward because there may be jealousy and resentment from them. They probably will not joke with you the way they used to when you go into a meeting. It's OK to continue to be friendly with them and to socialize with them, but understand that it will be a different relationship. Take time to be really clear about the new expectations even if it is a busy time. You can include them in defining how you will work as a team. Be conscientious about how you are going to lead in your new role. Do not allow yourself to fall into the trap of going to extremes to avoid losing them as friends."

The Payoffs of Forgiveness

The ultimate tool for dealing with conflict effectively is forgiveness. We were recording Doug Lennick when he was still the Executive

Vice President of American Express for our Learning From Experience™ series. One day, he clearly articulated the payoff of forgiveness. He started our recording session that day by saying, "Carol, I'd like to change our agenda today. I want to talk about forgiveness in the workplace. I'm finding more and more that forgiveness is a critical tool in the workplace, because anger takes so much energy to maintain that it significantly reduces productivity. Forgiveness is not about forgetting, it is not acquiescing; it is not ending your search for justice. It is simply letting go of the negative energy you are carrying around about that other person."

Forgiveness is not about forgetting, it is not acquiescing; it is not ending your search for justice. It is simply letting go of the negative energy you are carrying around about that other person.

Doug's comments inspired Carol to end a nine-year estrangement with her mother. She met with her mother to ask her forgiveness and to say goodbye. Her mother died three weeks later. Carol never regretted this choice to forgive and bring resolution to a challenging relationship.

So who are you angry with in your life? What thoughts are rolling through your brain and robbing you of peace? Forgiveness of yourself or others releases energy that can be available for more constructive thoughts and rebuild challenging relationships. It's never too late to forgive. In the words of Desmond Tutu, "Without forgiveness, there is no future."

C OMMAND

L EVERAGE

E XPECTATIONS

A UDIENCE

R ELATIONSHIP

L ISTENING

I NSPIRATION

8
LISTENING ENGAGEMENT

Listening is a major blind spot for many people, which limits their ability to have authentic executive presence. Few people are truly excellent listeners. However, many people believe they are good listeners.

Listening is an extremely important skill that we are able to help our clients significantly improve. Leaders who have excellent listening skills are very memorable.

Many years ago in Las Vegas, we experienced such a memorable leader. We were providing a keynote presentation for a large conference. As we spoke in the lobby of the hotel to two of the senior vice presidents of the firm hosting the conference, Bill, the Executive Vice President approached us. He introduced himself and told us how delighted he was with the work Change Masters was doing for the firm. He focused totally on us as a listener as he asked a few brief questions. Two minutes later, he moved, on wishing us good luck on our keynote—and we felt great. Bill had fully engaged with us and we still remember that two-minute encounter like it was yesterday. We instantly understood why people were willing to do whatever Bill needed them to do. You might not have his attention for very long because was so busy. But when he was with you, you were the only one that existed in his world. Bill demonstrated fantastic listening.

In this chapter, we will describe what is and is not good listening. We will expand on why listening is important and some techniques that our clients have found valuable for improving their abilities as a listener.

Traits of a Good Listener

We held a seminar with one of our customers where we asked the participants, "Who is the best listener you know?" Without hesitating, they all identified a single leader named Dan. The list of reasons they gave for selecting Dan as a good listener were that he:

Few people are truly excellent listeners.

- Had great eye contact.
- Pushed what he had aside to listen to you.
- Had great follow-up questions to seek understanding.
- Seemed relaxed even when you knew he had a lot going on.
- Had facial reactions, which helped you know where you were at with him.
- Used eye contact to really connect and focus on the speaker.
- Paused to think before he spoke, so you got a sense he really meant what he was about to say.
- Really sought to understand you.
- Showed many listening reactions, such as nodding and giving non-verbal responses, which told people how he felt about what they were saying.
- Committed himself to listening—he didn't multitask.

Then we asked the seminar participants, "How do Dan's behaviors make you feel?" They said:

- Dan cares about me.
- I'm important to him.
- I have his attention.
- He's approachable and accessible.
- My topic is his topic.
- I can make a difference.

Dan's exceptional listening also made people feel safe bringing issues to him early on to avoid surprises and solve problems before they became crises. How do you suppose these perceptions affected things like morale, productivity and retention in Dan's department? Enormously.

Good Listeners Are Busy, Too

The objection we often hear to improved listening is, "I just don't have time." Good listening skills actually save you time. When we met Bill in the lobby of the Las Vegas hotel, he only spent about two minutes with us, which was no more time than a perfunctory handshake and small talk. It was how Bill engaged that made the difference.

Good listening skills actually save you time.

Leaders who are great listeners are just as busy as anyone else, but they have learned to be fully present when they are listening. Even if it's just for two minutes, they make the speaker feel totally listened to.

Why Others Are Bad Listeners

People have no problem coming up with a long list of reasons why others are bad listeners. The list includes refusing to make eye contact or ignoring you; taking calls in the middle of a discussion; answering your questions before you finish because they think they know where you're going (even when they don't); multi-tasking on whatever electronic device is at hand or telling people, "You have thirty seconds—go."

Then there's our extreme example of terrible listening: it came from a senior executive of a technology company who sarcastically humiliated one of his key employees by abruptly interrupting his presentation in front of all his peers and saying, "That's enough, Jeff. Shut up and go lay down by your dog bowl." This single extraordinarily rude comment followed the executive until the day he retired—and beyond.

If listening integrity is so important to effective communications and the display of executive presence, why are so many people so mediocre at it? Well, here are some reasons we've heard from clients:

"I'm thinking about what I'm going to say."

"I want to talk first."

"You should understand that I agree. I don't have to tell you."

"I get it already."

"This is too hard to understand. I'm bored."

"I don't like you. I'm mad at you."

"I'm too distracted."

"I don't want to believe what I know you're about to tell me."

"I'd rather daydream or doodle."

Hearing Is Not Listening

Many people confuse "hearing" and "listening." Hearing is the physiological process of capturing information and filing it in your brain for future retrieval. An audio recorder can hear what is said to accurately record and retain the words. Many people think they are great listeners because they can remember precisely what was said.

What's the difference between hearing and listening? Listening is not just the absorption of information, but the emotional interaction and connection that authentically extends the relationship. Hearing is a subset of listening. Hearing is just the tennis ball and racquet, while listening is the full tennis game in which you keep the conversational ball in play back and forth across the net so people feel they have been respected in the process.

Visual Look of Listening

We use survey data and video recording to help our clients understand how they are perceived. It is a powerful way to see what it looks like to be sitting across the table from you as a listener. One of the most shocking things for most people to see is how indifferent, stone-faced or bored they look as listeners. The person they see is intimidating, cold and flat because all they're doing is processing what was said to them, but not effectively relating back to the person who is talking to them.

We often hear clients say "This is what my spouse has been telling me for years and I did not understand what he [or she] was talking about." Many people are so busy thinking that their face goes blank or may even look angry. The other person interprets the flat face in number of possible ways—none of them positive.

Survey data will describe characteristics of mediocre listeners as self-centeredness, indifference, not being strategic enough or being uncaring. Others feel blown off, de-motivated or bruised. Because you are powerful, it is even more significant to be aware of what your face and voice are doing at all times—it is the price of the power you hold.

Often when people have been told they need to improve their listening ability, they get worse. They confuse hearing and listening, because they concentrate more on intensely capturing the facts and not on building the relationship to let the other person know the impact of what was being said to them.

Great listening is the ability to pick up cues and read the room, to balance under- and over-participating in meetings so you neither dominate and annoy others, nor fade into the woodwork. People who give good non-verbal reactions while others are speaking stand out as engaged and intelligent. They are seen as good listeners.

Listening is Important

The Center for Creative Leadership has found that listening is the number-one success factor for senior executives. The test of a good listener is whether the other person feels heard and understood. Engaged listening is about understanding better what the speakers are really saying and connecting with them so they feel respected.

It is the responsibility of the listener to make the speaker feel understood as much as the other way around. When people have issues with you, it is often more important they feel you understand their view than it is that you agree with their view.

The higher you go in an organization, the more time you need to spend listening. Up to 60% of your day is spent listening when you're at executive levels, so you may as well be outstanding at it. Fortunately, significant improvement in listening effectiveness can be learned and successfully implemented. That is what Daniel found out.

Up to 60% of your day is spent listening when you're at executive levels, so you may as well be outstanding at it.

Listening Example—Blank Paper

Daniel was a regional president who was able to dramatically improve his listening skills and mentor others to enhance their skills also. Daniel was a brilliant man who had so many thoughts in his head he did not realize how he was plowing over people as they were trying to explain something to him. When we met him, he was a terrible listener—jumping in, interrupting and only focused on what he wanted to say. But Daniel became a student of great communications and a terrific listener.

Several years after completing his Change Masters coaching, Daniel advised Tim, a Vice President who had a similar listening issue. Daniel told Tim, "I know that you're annoyed with this group, as they are with you. I want you to be the bigger person. Start your next meeting with only this blank piece of paper. It represents the open mind I'd like you to have with them. Ask them just one question: 'What are your greatest concerns right now?' Write down everything they say to you. Don't defend, don't explain for the moment—only speak to draw them out more. Get every concern and irritation out on the table that you can. As much as is humanly possible, Tim, I'd like you to open your thinking toward them and truly listen to what they're telling you. I think you'll have an entirely different experience with them if you do." It was a watershed moment in how far Daniel had come in his listening competence as a senior leader and in his display of authentic executive presence.

Benefits to Great Listening

There are tremendous benefits to becoming a better listener beyond just displaying executive presence. Great listening:

Great listening builds trust.

- Builds trust.
- Gets issues resolved much faster.
- Opens you up in the eyes of others.
- Helps you more rapidly learn about the untold truths in the organization.
- Helps people feel valued by you and your organization, so it positively influences retention.
- Allows you to grow as a leader because you will learn about your blind spots and what you need to do to fix them.
- Helps you persuade others more effectively by quickly understanding their perspectives so you can address their concerns.

Like it or not, if you have position power you have more than half of the responsibility for successful communications. Listening engagement means gleaning the intent and emotions from what people are saying, not just the facts. The good news is that improving your listening by just a small degree will make a big difference. If you choose to be a great listener, you will be among a very elite group of leaders.

Listening as a Motivational Tool

One of the strong benefits of great listening is motivation. Marilyn Carlson Nelson is a great example of consistent, authentic executive presence, as well as excellent listening in her role as head of Carlson Companies. Some of her employees have described her level of listening engagement as "awe inspiring." One of them said, "When she's asked questions in a group setting or presentation, Marilyn doesn't just repeat the question, she acknowledges it, congratulates the speaker, recognizes the further challenges and summarizes them back to connect to her theme. Now that's great listening."

Generous listening is a gift that keeps on giving.

You can motivate tremendously, like Marilyn, through great listening, because generous listening is a gift that keeps on giving. It allows you to go to a second or even third level of depth of understanding and personal connection.

Listening with integrity requires that you listen for the factual data, the emotional intent and the contextual nuance. Listening for all three allows you to understand what you need to know early enough to take corrective action or unearth key influence factors. That's what Marilyn is doing in her public response to questions.

We advise our clients, even those who are in back-to-back meetings, to strive to stay engaged as listeners in every meeting they attend. Is it tough? Sure, but you're being paid for the whole day! The best way to do that is to start paying attention not just to the facts but also to people's emotional signals through their non-verbal reactions. There's a world of information out there, once you start to see it.

We've seen the very best listeners take an entire room of furious people and calm them down by the respectful manner in which they listen. Great listening separates you from the crowd, because so many people listen so poorly. We know—we see poor listeners all the time, and so do you.

Techniques that Make a Difference

Excellent listening requires hard work and emotional competence. It is a life-long journey. There are many proven practices that are relatively easy to implement that will improve your capability as a listener. The first step is to realistically assess how good you are as a listener and decide to make changes. There are a number of techniques that really help. Here are a few of them.

Bridge Statements

One key to being seen as a good listener is to let the speakers know that what they are saying has an effect on you. The bridge statement is an important part of sharing this impact.

> **One key to being seen as a good listener is to let the speakers know that what they are saying has an effect on you.**

Bridge statements are a way to connect what was just said to how it affected you intellectually or emotionally. Before you respond, you briefly tell them how you are impacted by their statement such as:

"You triggered a thought when you said…"

"I like that idea, Jim, because…"

"I'm frustrated because I thought we agreed last week to…"

"That is an intriguing way to look at this area. What if we…"

We've seen listening perceptions changed dramatically just by the effective use of bridge statements. They take virtually no time, but they increase the accuracy of understanding tremendously.

Without the bridge statements, people do not understand how your response ties to the importance of what they just said. As a result, they feel you were just waiting for your turn to talk and you were not listening.

It also gives you a chance to decide where you want to take the conversation next. One of our clients described telling his boss about the death of his mother, only to have her immediately start asking him questions about a proposal she was writing. Our client didn't even know how to begin to answer her. It left a lasting negative mark on the relationship.

Being more purposeful about using bridge statements builds a stronger relationship and increased authentic executive presence.

Visual and Vocal Listening Reactions

We described how to match your facial and vocal responses to your intent in Chapter Three. Those approaches also apply to listening. Your face is telling the other person your level of interest and your reaction. If there is no expression on your face, others tend to assume the worst possible reaction from you.

The visual expression and the tone of your voice when you respond have a large impact on how others interpret your reaction. One strong visual response to be aware of is rolling your eyes.

Marriage educators Sherri and Bob Pitrof note that rolling of the eyes is a frighteningly accurate in predicting the demise of a marriage relationship. It is a behavior that is seen in challenged workplace relationships as well. Eye rolling is seen as an end stage sign of exasperation, scorn, superiority, or a total lack of respect. No matter how tempting it can be to indulge in such behavior, realize that the cost of it at work intensifies hostility in your relationship because it creates reactions, which diminish trust, build power struggles and bring about withdrawal and defensive reactions.

Ask Great Questions

Good listeners also ask good questions. An insightful, interesting or unexpected question indicates the ability to move the conversation to the next level of complexity.

Ask one question at a time. When someone rattles off several questions at once without allowing for an answer, the other person feels attacked and assumes you really do not want an answer to any of the questions. Even worse, when stressed-out people are asked multiple rapid-fire questions in a harsh tone, they literally don't know which one to answer first. They become frozen in the headlights, momentarily paralyzed in their thought processing.

Remember that the semantic term for question is "interrogative," coming from the verb, "to interrogate." Any question, no matter how neutral your intent, has the potential to put people on the defensive if it's delivered incorrectly, so keep your voice calm and fairly flat in inflection when asking a question. The exception to this is when doing empathetic listening, in which you use a softer, warmer, more caring voice.

Here are some examples of great listening probe questions to draw others out:

> Any question, no matter how neutral your intent, has the potential to put people on the defensive if it's delivered incorrectly, so keep your voice calm and fairly flat in inflection when asking a question.

- What do you need most from me right now?
- Do you want any input right now, or do you just need to talk?
- What is your perspective?
- Can you help me understand what you're looking for?
- What would you do if you were in my shoes?
- What does this means to you?
- Why do you feel that way?
- What's an example of how that's impacting you?
- What are you hearing about this from others?
- How would you define success on this project?
- I can see you're concerned about this. What would make you more comfortable with this option?
- That's very different from what we expected. What happened?
- Can you ask me your question in a different way?
- That's terrific news! Can you tell me more about it?

- I know what you mean. I've been there myself. It's not easy, is it?
- No way... that's what they said? What happened next?
- I understand what you're saying. Any thoughts on what we need to do next?

Often, people just want to have you hear them out, so replace advice with curiosity. These listening questions can aid your perception significantly. It takes maturity to resist the temptation to jump in to fix problems just because you can, but it's worth it to maintain the relationship. A little time invested here will save you a great deal of time later.

Fillers

Speaking to a dismissive or a silent listener is very jarring. Frequently, listeners aren't nearly as negative as they appear to be. One way to make yourself be seen as more in line with your positive attitude is to use listening fillers. Fillers are one-word or one-phrase responses that give the speaker an indication that you're tracking with them. Variety is the key in making these responses sound authentic, not "canned" or phony. Try to use at least three different fillers when responding to people, as opposed to one repeated over and over. Vary them and stretch them out just a little longer to sound more engaged. Avoid rapidly repeating the same filler such as, "Yeah, yeah, yeah..." People see that as impatient and disengaged.

Use these phrases and words in either a normal speaking volume or "sotto voce," an Italian phrase meaning to speak under one's breath. Try some of these fillers as a way to expand your listening competence. It will be noticed and appreciated. Examples of phrases are:

- Really?
- Sure... that makes sense...
- That's right...
- Absolutely...
- OK...

- I understand…
- I see…
- Exactly…
- That's amazing…

They may seem superficial, but when you genuinely want to listen, they are very helpful for aligning your internal and external authenticity as a listener. Using a variety of fillers is a great tool to master.

Deal with Boredom

When you are bored in a meeting, everybody sees it. How do you respond when someone is talking about a topic that doesn't directly affect you? Do you check out? Do you pull out the hand held e-mail device or open up your computer? This is not the message you want to send on a regular basis, because trust us, people fool themselves by thinking they can multi-task while listening. It's universally seen as annoying and incredibly rude. We hear about it all the time in client data as a weakness needing to be corrected. Better to be honest and tell people you're exhausted, you're running late or you don't have time. Better yet, try listening to them.

Interruptions are not benign—they can be seen as annoying, rude, or condescending

To keep yourself constructively entertained as a listener, observe the interactive dynamics, think of the OPPOV questions (what are these people rewarded for, motivated by or afraid will happen), watch body language and see who's getting the best response from the group. Rather than sitting silently when you agree with only part of what's being said, figure out how you can demonstrate support for the elements you agree with by saying so. Get your thoughts out without dominating the conversation. It makes a significant impact in your perceived executive presence. It will make it easier to authentically deal with boredom in meetings.

Interruptions are not Benign

Interruptions are not benign—they can be seen as annoying, rude or condescending, because interrupters hijack control of the conversation. Interrupters seldom realize how often they interrupt. More importantly, they're unaware of how damaging their interruptions are to their effectiveness and relationships.

We've seen some company cultures that are tolerant of interruptions and some that don't appreciate it at all. There are also geographic and nationality differences in the propensity for interrupting. Interrupting tends to be more culturally acceptable in New York than in Minneapolis, Chicago than Atlanta and Boston than San Francisco. Granted, some people are oblivious to listening patterns and interruptions no matter where they live, but most are very sensitive to the impact of your listening style.

Here's how interruptions and a lack of listening reactions are seen by levels above, across and below you:

Superiors	Interruptions can be perceived by those above you as impulsive or immature.
Peers	Interruptions can be seen by those at equal levels as rude, out for yourself, annoying, political.
Subordinates	Interruptions can be seen by those below you as disliking or discounting them or their ideas, as an impatient, uncaring boss.

Granted, when people are excited, interruptions can naturally bubble up. On the whole, interruptions are seen as negative listening behavior.

Managing Your Time as a Listener

Many people pride themselves on their "open-door" policy. It's not novel, but the open door approach is often poorly executed. You have to be consistent when you tell people that if the door is cracked open, it's all right to disturb you for important questions. If you close your door, don't let people interrupt you. Ask them to come back later. If you're inconsistent with this policy, it will be violated.

Don't leave your door open and then resent being disturbed. Conversely, don't close your door most of the day and ignore the fact that dealing with appropriate interruptions is an important part of your job. When dealing with the interruptions at work or with your loved ones, be honest, respectful and when you listen, really be there.

To manage interruptions in a way that authentically represents how you want to be seen as a leader, first decide if you have time to truly listen or not. If you decide to listen, clear your mind, focus on the speaker, and truly listen. Physically push away from your desk or your computer and turn over or turn off your hand held e-mail device so you're not tempted to be distracted. Just making this choice to be more present gets you credit for being committed to listening and helps the other person feel heard.

Don't leave your door open and then resent being disturbed.

If a person just needs to vent, let them do so, but only for a specified time. Tell them in advance, "I have about 10 minutes... why don't you tell me what's going on?" If they need more time than that, arrange for them to come back later. If you decide this is not a good time to listen to them, schedule an alternate time when you can give your attention. Tell them, "I'm sorry, I can't give you the time you need right now. Can we get together at 3:00? I can spend more time then. Will that work for you?" Is the topic too big for a quick conversation? If so, you can say, "This seems like a larger topic than we can cover right now. Can you put this into a three-paragraph description and recommendation and set up a meeting with me next week so we can dig deeper?"

It's easy to be annoyed by all the interruptions to your work during the day and it's very natural to become overwhelmed by the many people who want to talk to you. The truth is that your interruptions are your work. So deal with them constructively.

Physical Engagement in Listening

One way to increase your executive presence as a listener is to manage your physical reactions. Calming your breathing pattern allows you to have the resources to deal more effectively with others as a listener. We call this "meeting breathing." It not only keeps you alert and awake, it helps you stay calm when the meetings you're sitting in (or conducting) are boring or frustrating. You can't change a physical reaction with a cognitive thought. You have to use a physical approach.

The truth is that your interruptions are your work. So deal with them constructively.

When under stress or irritated, your breathing becomes more rapid and shallow, further spurring adrenaline-based reactions. People under pressure breathe 12–22 times per minute! This verges on hyperventilation. As you sit in one of your many daily meetings, use them as an opportunity to recover from the stress you're under and slow down your breathing. When doing meeting breathing, extend the pattern. Inconspicuously inhale slowly and steadily for roughly five seconds and exhale for about five seconds. It immediately gives you a buffer so you can be more steady and clear in the moment, while keeping your sanity and your executive presence.

Be aware of your body during the day to be more effective as a listener. As we've noted before, your body will always win over your brain. You can squeeze your toes in your shoes during an annoying meeting moment and it will help you get through without saying something or doing something as a listener you'll later regret.

The 90/10 Rule

To conclude this chapter on listening we want to share a tool that works consistently to improve listening effectiveness, called the 90/10 Rule. When listening to an idea or proposal, it is very easy to go first to the problems or issues that may be of concern. When those are voiced, it sounds like you are disagreeing with the other person.

More often than not, you agree with 90% of what is being said, so the alternative is to start by saying, "Beth, I agree with 90% of what you are saying. We are completely aligned on that. I agree with what you are trying to accomplish with your proposal. I am concerned that we are not considering the reaction the sales representatives might have to this approach in terms of their compensation. I want to make sure we have a successful rollout, but I need to discuss our options on compensation further before I can get completely behind this." That way, you're starting from a place of connection, not separation, even though you're not totally aligned. Beth now has a better context for your concern.

One key to making this approach work well is the delivery tone of the message. It needs to be reasonably positive and not sound defensive or like an interrogation. The result will be that the other person feels heard even when you don't fully agree. You are then more likely to be able to work through an adjustment to your mutual satisfaction.

Remember, sometimes what you look like and sound like speaks so loudly others can't hear what you are saying. Make sure you know what message you are sending as a listener. Understand how others see you and hear you as a listener and you'll achieve tremendous authentic executive presence.

C OMMAND

L EVERAGE

E XPECTATIONS

A UDIENCE

R ELATIONSHIP

L ISTENING

I NSPIRATION

9

INSPIRATION, MOTIVATION AND PRAISE

People deliver best when they feel valued and respected, no matter what pressures exist. Organizations need people who are self-motivated and all moving in the right direction to thrive in an increasingly competitive global market. By using inspiration and praise to reinforce what you desire to achieve, you will be building your strongest competitive advantage. The increased stress in the workplace does not mean taking less time for recognition and praise. It means it is even more important than ever.

Unfortunately, many leaders are not very good at praise. Frequency and message delivery are the most frequent issues. Demonstrating honest warmth with engaged poise will make praise messages more effective, more authentic and more appreciated.

Payoffs of Courageous Praise

There's a great story about why geese honk to each other when they fly in their traditional "V" formation as they venture south. It's because the lead position at the top of the "V" is so exhausting, so physically tiring from the effort of slicing through the wind mile after mile, that the other geese honk at the lead goose simply to give it encouragement to keep going. The same needs for reinforcement exist for those above, below and across from you. Once they get it from you, they're much more likely to give some of that reinforcement back to you—free of charge!

Let's start this chapter on authentic praise, motivation and inspiration with some situations in which it can go awry or get lost. Most professionals have absolutely no idea how others perceive the way they praise. They far overrate their competence to inspire and amount of praise they give. Why? Because they aren't matching what they feel on the inside with what people hear, see and experience from them on the outside. Some fear "spoiling" their people with praise. Still others don't take the time to inspire or motivate because they're so focused on results. Such was the case with Janell.

The increased stress in the workplace does not mean taking less time for recognition and praise. It means it is even more important than ever.

When we met her, Janell was an introverted, highly driven CEO of a large East Coast hospital system. She had started her career years earlier as an emergency room nurse. She advanced in the organization by taking on a tough, hard persona, because she thought she had to emulate her male counterparts. She had always been articulate and direct, but now as CEO, these same characteristics were seen as inflexible, intimidating and indifferent. When we met Janell, she was being called "the barracuda" behind her back.

People were terrified to make mistakes because she would crush them in public. Janell was achieving the results, but she was seen as extremely intimidating. In her first coaching session with us, she realized she had lost touch with the caring, human side that had originally led her into nursing. She was saddened and shocked but determined to change. It turned out to be a transformational experience for Janell, one that later set her up for a number of major promotions.

Janell courageously choose to tell her Board of Directors that she was committing to do the following actions:

- Spend more time inspiring, less time perspiring.
- Be tough on expectations, but tender on people.
- Truly delegate—let others take the lead instead of plowing over them if they aren't instantly on target.
- Praise for progress, not just for perfection.
- Simplify my message and make it warmer.
- Spend time connecting to be more approachable.
- Get out of my head and re-connect to my heart.
- Have people feel like they could make mistakes and survive.

One of the things that greatly influenced Janell was the concept of "de-but-ing" praise. She would say, "Great job, but…" so her praise didn't get heard.

> **Most professionals have absolutely no idea how others perceive the way they praise.**

Janell later told us, "I now know that to get others to communicate, I have to model it for them. If I let others assume too many things about me, they'll probably assume incorrectly."

Janell realized that as CEO, she had a lot of power she was misusing. She noted, "I've seen it proven ever since coaching that when you can blend task and relationship, you feel better about yourself. Self-awareness recharges your battery so you can enjoy what you're doing more. Just smiling at people more has made a difference for me and for my team—it's fascinating how a physical act like smiling can change your mental mindset. Most importantly, I feel like I have more energy today. I never realized how much my intensity was driving out my joy."

This powerful, courageous woman went on to be promoted to lead multiple large hospital systems in even bigger roles of responsibility over the years and was able to contribute her skills to the organization for well over a decade. Janell inspired and motivated people every step of the way. We felt privileged to be part of that journey to help develop her authentic executive presence.

Gracious Recovery From Mistakes

We have worked with many high-potential groups in global companies to help them see themselves as others do. A common approach is where we help the participants display executive presence in preparation for their upcoming presentations to their Executive Committee. After the participants video recorded the openings of their presentations, we coach them to display more poise under pressure.

It's ironic— sometimes you can actually achieve a greater perception of authentic executive presence when you blow it and recover than if you did it right the first time!

At the end of one such seminar, we had them all vote on who had displayed the most courageous display of executive presence. One of the participants, Barry, thought he would be the laughingstock of his peer group because of how he had messed up, yet he ended up being voted the most courageous participant of them all.

Barry was a native New Yorker who had enthusiastically proclaimed he really wanted to see himself on camera. When he stood up in front of the group the first time, however, he became flustered. Barry had memorized his script. He was so nervous that when we asked him one simple question before he spoke, it completely threw him and his mind went blank. He froze and he forgot everything he was trying to say in front of his peers—twice.

Despite this inauspicious start, when we did his live coaching Barry showed a tremendous turnaround through his tenacity. By the time we were done with coaching, he displayed relaxed confidence and presence. His peers not only applauded his achievement, they gave him a standing ovation. It was a master class in how to recover from a setback in order to inspire others. It's ironic—sometimes you can actually achieve a greater perception of authentic executive presence when you blow it and recover than if you did it right the first time!

Praise Under Pressure

We learn a lot about people by how they handle themselves when they're angry or under pressure. Robert McNamara, when he was Secretary of Defense under President John Kennedy, complained that he didn't have a road map to follow or any precedent for certain actions he was being asked to take in the Cuban missile crisis. Kennedy exasperatedly declared to McNamara, "Bob, there's no manual for how to be President, either!"

> Leadership effectiveness decreases by 50% if you blow up just once every six months.

When you're feeling unappreciated, uncertain or under-recognized, it is easy to get a chip on your shoulder, which affects your effectiveness and perception as a leader. When you're feeling this way, it's tough to reinforce others. Part of executive presence and leadership maturity is to choose your response under pressure and take full accountability for those choices. This is critical, because studies show that your leadership effectiveness decreases by 50% if you blow up just once every six months. People walk on eggshells around you to avoid having it happen again.

Use impulse control and be purposeful when you're ticked off. Avoid at all costs the approach a client described as his previous style when frustrated and under pressure, "Shoot the bazookas and cannons at them—rifles would be too kind!" Fortunately, this same man learned to show a more mature approach to frustration while incorporating a motivational, inspirational approach. He's been so successful that today he is sought out company-wide to tell his story to emerging leaders about moving from being an emotional train wreck to demonstrating gracious engagement and motivation under pressure.

The average corporate executive is markedly sleep-deprived, having the alertness level between 2:00–4:00 P.M. of a 75-year-old! You can't motivate others unless you're taking care of yourself. You can't show emotionally mature poise if your exhaustion causes you to be living on the ragged edge.

> **When a senior executive gives a compliment, it is remembered for a minimum of 16 months after the original event!**

Suppose two employees have the same results, but one takes seventy hours a week to get it done and looks stressed, frazzled and frustrated. The other employee takes fifty hours a week to get the same things done, and seems to make it look easy. Who gets the promotion?

Too many people think if they work long hours they should be rewarded, but you have to give the promotion to the person who has more capacity. Taking care of yourself so you can demonstrate motivational and inspirational prowess are more effective ways to get results than turning yourself into road kill. You can't display executive presence or give authentic praise on an empty tank.

The Power of Meaningful Praise

Studies tell us that when a senior executive gives a compliment, it is remembered for a minimum of 16 months after the original event! People keep a file of the positive e-mails you send or the notes you write to them, sometimes for years. What else gives you such a positive return on your investment of 30 seconds?

Many people actually leave their jobs for the single, simple reason that they don't feel they receive enough recognition. Their leaders might have thought they were doing a great job, but they didn't tell them often enough—or ever.

A painful truth, however, came from one of our clients. He said, "You know, I can't remember the last one-on-one I had with my boss. It makes me wonder, 'Do I matter? Am I significant?' I know that it doesn't mean she doesn't care—it's just the job and being overbooked, I know, but it still makes me wonder." This is not a great retention strategy! Your notes, letters and e-mails affect people more than you can ever imagine.

In a recent survey of nearly 8,000 employees, 48% said they suffer from a lack of feedback on their performance and 69% of those who felt they weren't receiving feedback were thinking of looking for another job. Some leaders have an attitude of, "If you're not hearing from me, you're OK. No news is good news." This approach is just not going to cut it with your kids or your employees. The replacement costs of an employee today are easily twice his or her annual salary. The lesson here? Don't be stingy with your compliments.

Praise is the most powerful form of all communication. Meaningful, authentic praise makes people want to follow you and stay through hard times. We've heard time and again that the reason a person is staying with a company is because of Joanne or Cynthia or Mark.

Dave, one of Carol's in-house legal clients, became a leader who really expanded his praise-giving ability. Lawyers aren't exactly taught how to praise and motivate in law school, so this was quite an achievement for him. It was very heartening to see such expanded awareness from Dave because it had previously been extremely difficult for him to praise people. There were several reasons for this resistance:

- He was incredibly tough on himself, and his high standards caused everyone to fall short of what he expected.

- He feared sounding like he had gone to charm school or a seminar on praising and it would sound contrived.

- He had a boss in the past who overdid all his praise, saying things like "You're amazing!" to the smallest things. Dave didn't trust the boss' intent or agenda, so he went the opposite direction and rarely praised at all.

There is a middle ground for praise. It doesn't have to be overblown and fake or totally withheld. Carol reminded Dave that he really valued the praise he got from his current boss, Alex. When asked why, Dave said, "Alex is smart, he gets me, he's successful and makes it clear that he values what I bring to the table. I keep learning from him."

Statistics show most employees want to please their bosses but they don't always know how. Praise is a way to tell them what you want them to repeat so they can do that and be successful with you. Telling them what you like about what they did means they'll be more likely to give it to you again. That's a subtle purpose of the praise and motivation messages that most people miss. Giving praise improves productivity because you get more of what you reinforce—it's as simple as that.

I Believe in You

A client of ours who was a Vice President of Sales and Marketing learned how one great, heart-felt motivational talk at the right time could take a group out of a paralyzed state. He asked us to help him craft a message he needed to give to his devastated team shortly after the World Trade Center tragedy of 9/11. His team feared for their industry and their jobs after this terrible catastrophe. This is an excerpt from the close of his talk.

"I want to close by reading you a few sentences from a book a good friend gave to me recently. I'm not one who usually enjoys those little books of quotes, but this one called *I Believe in You*, by Dan Zada, really struck me. It says,

In the game of life, maybe we should always be strong enough and sure enough to go it alone. Maybe it shouldn't matter whether someone else believes in us or not—but it does. There will always be many experts who can give us all the reasons why we shouldn't, we won't or we can't. That's why we cherish those rare individuals who are there to remind us why we should, why we will, why we can. And this has always been so.

Two thousand years ago, a 17-year-old Egyptian girl wrote this message to her mother on a ragged piece of papyrus that is still preserved in the Metropolitan Museum of Art: "Dear Mother, I'm all right. Stop worrying about me. Start believing in me."

It was true then, and it's true now. All human progress has been the story of someone who believed passionately in something, and someone who believed passionately in that person.

"I was very moved by that passage," said the Vice President, "because it reminds me how important it is that you know how much I believe in each one of you in this room. Now, I need you to believe in yourself and in the power you have to reinvent yourself. Believe in each other and in what we can achieve together... because, my friends... I believe in you. That's what I want you to remember today, after all the facts and figures have left your head, just remember this one thing—that I believe in you."

This speech moved the group to tears. It was just what they needed to hear to keep moving ahead in an uncertain time. This leader's choice to open up and show his vulnerability and strength allowed his team to move to a different place and become functional in an uncertain time.

Have Fun!

Showing your gratitude, whether it's in a moment of pain or in a lighthearted manner, is a key to the display of executive presence.

You'll never go wrong by showing your sincere thanks and respectfully having some fun with your team in the workplace. You never lose by giving more praise. All you do is gain loyalty, hope and perseverance.

You'll never go wrong by showing your sincere thanks and respectfully having some fun with your team in the workplace.

Jack had been a great project manager earlier in his career. When we met, he had 250 technology professionals reporting to him, scattered around the world. It was very tough for him to motivate them because he was so self-motivated. He had never needed much reinforcement from any of his leaders. He forgot about reinforcing others.

Jack's survey said he had a major issue with team morale. To counter this perception we had Jack do a very deliberate strategic praise plan for 90 days. One of the most successful parts of the plan was the 5:5:15 approach.

All it entailed was for Jack to send out a message once a week, on Friday afternoons (the fifth day of the week) at 5:15, when he had a moment of time free. He sent his employees a quick update on how the week had gone, told them where he'd be and what he'd be doing in the next week and ended with a joke, an inspiring quote or a message of praise and inspiration. It took him maybe ten minutes and it got a huge response from his team.

One week Jack couldn't write the e-mail and he heard about it from half his staff! They had come to rely on the praise and status communication tool that took so little time from Jack, but reassured and recognized his staff. Here is an e-mail example:

From: Jack Mann
Sent: Friday, August 31, 20XX
To: Marketing User Group
Subject: Weekly Update

Team,

Wow! What a hectic week! Because it's been so hectic lately, I know it's been difficult to get hold of me, and I wanted to take a moment to get us all on the same page, and to thank you for your great work.

Thanks so much for pulling together this week on the Acme business case, the Robertson testing & evaluation, and with our continued push to achieve Miami's aggressive goals. I've been very impressed with your efforts and very grateful for them.

I know this is a time of transition for us, and that can cause anxiety—especially when we haven't yet settled on how our new teams will be staffed for the projects ahead. I assure you everything is going to be OK. In fact, more than OK.

By now, each of you has discussed with your supervisor or with me the work we have ahead of us and how it aligns with your own particular interests. We're doing everything we can to align those interests with what we need to accomplish. I'll discuss them with you in our group meeting on Wednesday of next week.

Don't be intimidated by the uncertainty or the huge challenges ahead of us. We've been given these challenges because of who you are and because of your track record of success. Taking on big hard things is what we do, and our new staffing levels will allow us to succeed while maintaining our work/life balance. If that balance ever deteriorates, come see me and I'll get us back on track. I promise.

I've been with General Companies for over 7 years and I've never been more excited.

Jack

We had Jack send us a copy of his weekly communiqués to his team so we could act as his accountability partner as he incorporated this motivation tactic into his weekly routine. This approach worked so well for Jack that it became self-perpetuating, as he told us several weeks later:

> Hope you're doing well. These 5:5:15 messages have been a hit with my team—been getting unsolicited praise about them from all levels of my organization and I have you to thank for it.
>
> The praise has been so consistent, and the benefits so clear, that I feel confident I'll continue this without an accountability partner, so I'm going to stop forwarding these to you. I'll be forever grateful that you got me started on it. Thanks so much—
>
> Jack

As you can see, the 5:5:15 gives a badly needed dose of fun and energy. Having fun and perspective makes the day go better for each of us. A light, appropriate touch of humor can work wonders for your executive presence. We were talking to a senior executive of a highly profitable, rapidly growing company and asked him, "How's life in the fast lane, Paul?" He responded, "It's great, if you can keep the car on the highway!" You don't need to be hysterically funny, you just need to give people a sense of perspective and put them at ease.

A feeling of fun is something Tom Debrowski of Mattel believes in completely. He says, "True leaders never take themselves too seriously. It's easy to get wrapped up in the big title, the big office, the company car, all that stuff. Come on, get a life! Realize that all of that stuff can be undone in a heartbeat and it will be, because one day you'll be gone and somebody else will be doing your job.

"So relax; you're blessed to be in the role for this moment only. You're probably only in the role because of a string of wonderful experiences and great people who helped you get where you are.

Don't ever let your ego forget that. Lighten up! Fun is infectious—spread it around. Encouraging fun builds relationships and the depth, quality and enduring nature of these relationships depends on what you bring to work every day and what you're willing to share."

The 5:1 Ratio

Many of our clients initially see themselves as giving much more positive feedback than others experience from them. Most people treat giving praise to those around them in the workplace as a rare and unusual thing, only necessary in extraordinary circumstances. One of our earliest clients was a man who oversaw a six-billion-dollar international meat packing organization. He was grumbling after reading in his data that his people saw him as only begrudgingly giving praise. He muttered, "I pay them. Do I have to praise them, too?" Yes, you do—and it will be even truer with upcoming generations of employees and leaders.

I pay them. Do I have to praise them, too? Yes, you do—and it will be even truer with upcoming generations of employees and leaders.

We've actually had clients say, "I don't praise people because I don't want them to get lazy. If I praise them for every little thing, they'll just stop trying." One of our clients feared the opposite—if he praised his people too much, he'd be seen as weak and his people would take advantage of him. Perhaps a few people are like this, but if you let the vast majority of people who work for you know clearly what you want and then praise them clearly for giving you what you want, you'll get more of what you desire. The concept of, "It means more if I say it less" when it comes to praise and motivation just doesn't work with the attitudes, needs and perceptions of those coming into the workplace today.

Studies have found that the average working adult needs five positive indicators (vocal, visual and content messages) for every one critical indicator received just for them to believe that you think they're OK. We call this the 5:1 ratio. Kids need up to ten positive indicators for every critical indicator. Many people reverse this praise ratio in the workplace and at home: they give one positive indicator for every five critical indicators.

To give effective praise, be specific—tell them exactly what you liked about what they gave you. That way they're more likely to repeat the behavior and give you more of what you want. Connect the praise back to the actions as quickly as possible. A great approach for this is the "Feeling/Reason/Action" approach noted in Chapter Three. Tell them how their actions made you feel, why you feel that way and what actions you want them to repeat. Direct praise helps people keep buying in to your requests for them to do more, but it has to be very customized. That's why we created the Praise Matrix.

The Praise Matrix

Positive messages have huge payoffs for most individuals, but they need to work for their own personal style. There are some people who want a quiet pat on the back, accompanied by a large check in a plain white envelope. Others want a billboard erected in their honor! However, most people enjoy lingering in the moment of recognition.

Giving praise works best when it is timely and specific, but also when it's customized. Give praise in the manner most beneficial to the receiver. Face-to-face, in writing or publicly, each method has its own benefits, but the impact of praise increases dramatically when done in a manner that works best for the person who is receiving it. That's what the Praise Matrix can help you find out. It helps you find out how they like to get it, or in what form it should be.

Our Praise and Recognition Matrix is a guide in how to do this. It separates praise and recognition according to how a specific individual best likes to receive it in a customized manner that works for them.

We ask our clients to use this matrix with their people or their peers, leaders or other centers of influence.

Getting Credit for Praise Through Delivery That Works for Them

	CALM ENERGY IN THE DELIVERY	HIGHLY ENERGIZED IN THE DELIVERY
DELIVERED IN PUBLIC MANY OTHERS KNOW ABOUT IT	Fred Josh Carrie	Maria Jack
DELIVERED IN PRIVATE OTHERS DON'T KNOW ABOUT IT	Jackie Robert Bill	Gary

Put the name of your team member, peer or upper manager in the box that most closely describes how you think they'd like to get praise. You can even ask them if you got it right—it is guaranteed to give you a fascinating conversation. After all, who doesn't like to have someone think about them in terms of how they'd like to be praised?

It is appropriate to discuss your categorization with the individuals to confirm or deny your assessment. This discussion can work both ways. You can also tell them what works for you in the area of praise by putting yourself on the matrix. It's something they'd like to know and you're the only one who knows how to accurately tell them.

Inform Your Face!

No matter what approach people need, you won't go wrong if you project energy that is more positive. Lighten up your delivery to show your enthusiasm for what you or your group is doing. Inform your face and voice that you're happy, and your energy will be contagious, while still being credible.

To get full credit for giving praise, vary not only the message but also the delivery of your praise based on the style and preference of the individual. Smile, or at least relax your face! We will often do a freeze frame when watching the playback of a praise moment from a client and ask, "Are you praising them or firing them? Because I can't tell the difference—and if I can't, neither can they. As a result, your praise efforts are going to be in vain."

Inform your face and voice that you're happy, and your energy will be contagious, while still being credible.

To get full credit for your praise, try showing the following visual and vocal delivery behaviors:

Use an upbeat, overtly excited demeanor by:

- Vocally, hit the high notes—use more notes on the oscilloscope.
- Inform with your face that you're happy! Show warmth, possibility and interest in your face. Smile broadly and consistently.
- Raise up your brow—don't look surprised, just interested.

To have authentic charisma, warmth and lightness, to give inspiration at work, you need to keep your engagement high, the connections strong and be willing and able to keep perspective and a healthy sense of humor, even when the pressure is on.

In addition to the visual and vocal aspects of praise, remember that there are five phrases that just aren't said often enough in the workplace, which can really make a difference in how you're seen as a leader. They are:

1. "Thank you."
2. "I appreciate you."
3. "How are you really doing?"
4. "What do you need from me?"
5. "I'm sorry."

You can start saying these things significantly more often today to get credit for having emotional depth. They're free, they're quick and they work!

Just Do It!

A respected, analytical and somewhat introverted Vice President from a Fortune 500 company told us recently, "Executive presence is all about relationships. People will forget what you said or did but will never forget how you made them feel. I had to learn this over the years. It took me a long time to realize that it was not only OK, it was essential to be social at work.

It finally dawned on me, 'Why don't you just tell them they did a really good job? It makes them feel good and it's all true.'

"Early on as a leader, I never talked about my family—I was turning into an overbearing, serious ogre. When I got feedback on that, I started working on opening up about myself in a staff meeting. My Human Resource leader came up to me later and said, 'The stories you shared about yourself were excellent. I learned more about you in the last 40 minutes than I did in the last two years! You were always so serious before. You never talked about how much you loved baseball or golf before. You're actually a pretty nice guy!'

"It finally dawned on me, 'Why don't you just tell them they did a really good job? It makes them feel good and it's all true!' When I started to do that, they started calling me 'the new guy'—even though I've worked here 22 years! This really showed up when we had a lunch for Sheila, one of my employees who was going on maternity leave. I stood up and told the group that Sheila was creative as hell, she could boil a 20-page report down to one page with perfect clarity and how she helped transform our group to be more cost-effective. I ended by saying, 'Sheila, you have no idea the positive impact you have on people.' Sheila sat there with her mouth open, and then she started to tear up! She said that meant so much to her because she never knew whether I approved of her work or of her before. When I heard that, I realized, 'Wow, I could be way more effective if I did this more often.' I used to believe that people would trust my praise more if I didn't do it as often, so I didn't toss it around haphazardly.

"The other reason I didn't praise, though, was that I really didn't know what to say to people. Janey, my assistant, was retiring, so she felt free to say what was on her mind. She told me, 'Look, they'll listen to anything you say because you're the boss! Just get out there and talk to these people! You're intimidating them because they don't know how they feel about you and they're reading meaning into everything you do. Just try to connect with them. Tell them why you like what they're doing. They're hungry for it. Say anything!'

"I learned to go out with a cup of coffee and make the rounds with people, or call them up and say hello, confer, ask about their kids or their interests. I'll never be great at it, but I know they appreciate my attempts."

Asking For Help and Surviving

We leave you with a story that demonstrates inspiration, emotional competence and executive presence in a slightly different way. A Director-level client of ours, Josh, learned how to demonstrate poise under pressure in a way he never expected. Josh had hit a place in his life where he really needed help from others, with something that was too big for him to possibly control.

Josh worked incredibly hard at his job, and he was a great person—if a peer or team member was sick, he helped them in a heartbeat. When the situation was reversed, however, it never occurred to him that he could—and should—ask for their help. Sound familiar?

Josh hadn't been feeling well, and he kept putting off finding out why because he was too busy working. When he finally saw a doctor, he was shocked to learn that he had to have surgery for a large brain tumor. The tumor was in a very tricky place in his brain, and the only surgeons with a successful record of accomplishment for this type of tumor were at Johns Hopkins University.

Josh was used to having his work output and quality define much of who he was as a professional. This perspective was very deeply ingrained in Josh. So we asked him to consider trading on the credibility capital he had built with others.

In a similar manner, we each have built-up credibility capital that we can and must trade upon when the going gets tough. There are those you work with right now who have a negative balance in the credibility or trust account that they have with you. They don't have much capital to trade upon. Then there are those who you know will go to the ends of the earth to get things accomplished. That was Josh.

They said they'd worked harder than ever so I wouldn't have to worry.

Josh had worked hard to turn around his team in earlier, challenging times. He had supported them, had demonstrated remarkable personal and professional growth, and was now well-respected for the leadership he had shown. He now had to understand that he could tap into the capital that respect bought him in order to cope with the physical trauma that was coming his way. As a proud man, it was tough for him to seek out this type of help. It felt like weakness to him, but he was running out of options.

We encouraged Josh to tell those around him what he was facing. He started to let people know how he really felt about what was to happen to him, about his fears and his hopes for a full recovery. In a calm and sincere manner, he told his team, his peers and those above him that the uncertainty of this surgery and subsequent treatment had taken more of an emotional toll on him than he had ever anticipated.

Josh told them how they could help him, by simply "being an ear to my fear" as he put it, and reassured them to not be afraid or avoid him just because of this health crisis. He asked them to reach out to him, to send him e-mails or cards. Even if they didn't know what to say, he just wanted to know that they were thinking of him.

We encouraged Josh to ask his team to take on some extra work assignments, preparing them in advance for his extended absence while he was still available to give input.

And what was the response? People at all levels were over-whelmingly positive in telling Josh how they supported him. In fact, it was so positive that Josh later told us, "This is blowing me away—it is so contrary to all my beliefs on what people would think of me if I showed this type of vulnerability. They told me this had actually motivated them more than anything we'd ever done as a group. They said they'd worked harder than ever so I wouldn't have to worry.

"I had been afraid to tell them because I thought they'd see me as weak. I mean, not only was I not rejected, they told me that they were actually able to relate to me more as a person. As a result of what I asked of them, they had a concrete way of showing me that they supported me, and they actually thanked me for the chance to help in a situation where they wouldn't have known how to do so in a meaningful way!"

It was the last thing Josh expected, and it was exactly what he needed. The inspired reaction of his team gave Josh the capacity to deal with things he couldn't have dealt with before. They motivated him to work even harder in his rehabilitation process. The motivation worked both ways.

Despite a challenging recovery from brain surgery during which he literally had to learn how to walk and move again, the great news is that Josh fully recovered from a successful set of surgeries to remove his brain tumor. His newfound optimism and gratitude for all the support he'd received caused him to be a different man. He grew tremendously in his career following this experience and his experience inspired many others to step up their leadership as well.

Why wait for a health crisis to realize that you can't do it all yourself, that you might actually have to ask for help? Why wait for a trauma to show people you're human, to connect with them? Why not start now to be more open, more human and more real with those around you at work?

Sometimes it seems like our clients believe that when they walk through the doors of their workplaces, they pass through some kind of invisible membrane that strips them of their emotions and vulnerabilities. Yet, as Josh found, nothing could be further from the truth. We are all human beings, not human doings, at work; human beings who are made up of logic and intellect and fears and joys and insecurities. Josh realized he didn't have to work so hard to hide those parts of him when he asked others for their help, and in so doing, he gained productivity, team loyalty and a tremendous amount of versatility that made him a much more effective leader. Let yourself share more of who you are at work and ask for help when you really need it. You'll gain tremendous authenticity, emotional and motivational capital—without having to go under the knife.

Succeeding In Seeing Yourself As Others Do

All of the CLEARLI approaches can be implemented immediately, but very few people excel at all of them simultaneously. When you can enhance just a few of these attributes consistently, however, you will achieve a major lift in how you are perceived. By CLEAR-LI *Seeing Yourself as Others Do* using all seven attributes, even relatively well, you will be a leader people will remember for the rest of their lives.

When asked what type of ending he preferred in a movie, director and producer Steven Spielberg replied with one word, "Hope." It is our hope that this book has given you some insight on how to see yourself as others do and practical, pragmatic approaches to manage your perception by incorporating more facets of authentic executive presence.

On this journey, there are no easy answers. There is no silver bullet. There is only you, your talents and your commitment. With that, you cannot fail.

Go to www.ExecutiveCoach.com for
"World class coaching delivered around the world."

- Global executive presence
- Managing/communicating with remote teams
- Group remote learning
- Individual remote learning
- Digital/internet tools
- Videoconferencing presence

Go to www.ChangeMasters.com
or email info@ChangeMasters.com
for additional information on:

- Individual Coaching
- Group Coaching
- Presentation Coaching
- Team Development
- Keynotes
- Workshops and Seminars
- CLEARLI Assessments

Go to www.SeeingYourselfAsOthersDo.com to:

- Tell us your stories about executive presence and read more stories (the best and worst examples)
- Submit your questions or view frequently asked questions
- View updated information
- Sign up for newsletters and electronic feeds

Introduction

Foundation

Command

Leverage

Expectations

Audience

Relationship

Listening

Inspiration

Next Steps